Aldridge, Rebecca.
Stella McCartney /
2011

JUN

 W9-CTM-213

37565020145388

cent

FAMOUS
FASHION
DESIGNERS

STELLA McCARTNEY

FAMOUS FASHION DESIGNERS

COCO CHANEL

MARC JACOBS

CALVIN KLEIN

RALPH LAUREN

STELLA McCARTNEY

ISAAC MIZRAHI

VALENTINO

VERSACE

FAMOUS
FASHION
DESIGNERS

STELLA McCARTNEY

Rebecca Aldridge

CHELSEA HOUSE
An Infobase Learning Company

STELLA McCARTNEY
Copyright © 2011 by Infobase Learning

Chelsea House
An imprint of Infobase Learning
132 West 31st Street
New York NY 10001

Library of Congress Cataloging-in-Publication Data

Aldridge, Rebecca.
　Stella McCartney / by Rebecca Aldridge.
　　p. cm. — (Famous fashion designers)
　Includes bibliographical references and index.
　ISBN 978-1-60413-982-2 (hardcover)
　1. McCartney, Stella, 1971-　　—Juvenile literature. 2. Fashion designers—England—Biography—Juvenile literature. 3. Women fashion designers—England—Biography—Juvenile literature.　I. McCartney, Stella, 1971-　　II. Title.
　TT505.M34A43 2011
　746.9'2092—dc22
　[B]　　　　　　2010033972

Chelsea House books are available at special discounts when purchased in bulk quantities for businesses, associations, institutions, or sales promotions. Please call our Special Sales Department in New York at (212) 967-8800 or (800) 322-8755.

You can find Chelsea House on the World Wide Web at
http://www.chelseahouse.com

Text design and composition by Lina Farinella
Cover design by Alicia Post
Cover printed by Bang Printing, Brainerd, Minn.
Book printed and bound by Bang Printing, Brainerd, Minn.
Date printed: February 2011
Printed in the United States of America

10 9 8 7 6 5 4 3 2 1

This book is printed on acid-free paper.
All links and Web addresses were checked and verified to be correct at the time of publication. Because of the dynamic nature of the Web, some addresses and links may have changed since publication and may no longer be valid.

Contents

Introduction: More than Just a Name   6

1   A "Normal" Childhood   10

2   The Fashion-World Fledgling   18

3   Reinvigorating Chloé   26

4   Gucci's New Girl   37

5   Success in Work, Life, and Love   50

6   The Brand Branches Out   63

7   Activist and Advocate   74

8   McCartney Continues Making Her Way   83

Chronology and Timeline   94
Glossary   98
Bibliography   100
Further Resources   107
Picture Credits   108
Index   109
About the Author   112

More than Just a Name

It is the evening of October 20, 2000, and Kid Rock is onstage getting the audience pumped by performing his own rendition of the Rolling Stones classic "Jumpin' Jack Flash" at the opening of the VH1/Vogue Fashion Awards. The Theater at New York's Madison Square Garden is packed. Other performers, like Destiny's Child, Macy Gray, and Lenny Kravitz, take their turns heating up the stage. During the lively ceremony, cohosts—model Gisele Bündchen and Academy Award–winning actor Cuba Gooding Jr.—exchange banter and ultimately look cool; since fashion is the theme of the evening, the two change ensembles a total of 12 times between them.

On hand as presenters at the gala event are a who's who of celebrity fashion mavens and designers themselves: Uma Thurman, Donatella Versace, Renee Zellweger, Tom Ford, Courtney

Love, Elizabeth Hurley, Natalie Portman, and Milla Jovovich. The list of winners for the evening is studded with stars as well: No Doubt for Most Stylish Video, Macy Gray for Most Fashionable Artist—Female, Enrique Iglesias for Most Fashionable Artist—Male, Chloë Sevigny for Celebrity Style—Female, and Jude Law for Celebrity Style—Male.

Actress Liv Tyler is busy hanging out with friend and fashion designer Stella McCartney; in fact, she is wearing a jumpsuit that had just made its debut only weeks before at the runway show for the new Chloé collection created by the French label's creative director, McCartney herself.

The British designer is attending the award show as a nominee for one of the evening's most prestigious honors: Designer of the Year. For this award, nominees are selected by a committee of top fashion editors, journalists, curators, stylists, designers, photographers, and models put together by VH1 and *Vogue*. The Designer of the Year winner is then determined by votes cast on both the Vogue.com and VH1.com Web sites. The previous year, nominees were all prominent names in the business: Gucci, Calvin Klein, Donna Karan, Giorgio Armani, and Ralph Lauren. Some of McCartney's competition this year is no different and includes fashion industry veterans like Calvin Klein and Miuccia Prada.

McCartney's chances seem slim; she is a relative neophyte who has been out of design school for only five years. The name called this year, however, is not one of the more iconic fashion names. Instead, heralded to the stage is the new 2000 Designer of the Year, Stella McCartney for Chloé, and there to present it to her proudly is father—and music legend—Paul McCartney. Stella is taken by surprise. "I had no idea he was coming here," she told *Entertainment Weekly*, "[a]nd I'm a bit freaked out."

In only five years, McCartney had come a long way—from fashion school grad to design chief of Chloé. And within another five years, she'd go even further. She would become known in the

When Stella McCartney accepted the VH1/Vogue Designer of the Year Award, her father, musician Paul McCartney, surprised her by wearing a T-shirt with the message "About Flippin' Time." The shirt was a nod to the one Stella wore when Paul was inducted into the Rock and Roll Hall of Fame.

sometime ruthless world of fashion as Stella Steel for her remarkable combination of ambition and determination. The rich and famous would wear her designs around London and the world, including friends and fans like Kate Moss, Madonna, Natalie Portman, Scarlett Johansson, and even Zara Phillips, Queen Elizabeth's granddaughter.

McCartney has often said that she designs what she likes and what both she and her friends like to wear, and that taste must extend to the everywoman because her collections are high in demand. Beginning with her collections for Chloé and even as she stepped away to begin her own label, her designs, including tops that can equal the cost of a flat-screen television, have become known for their eminently wearable quality.

Her friends include show-business luminaries, many of whom, like McCartney herself, were the children of well-known entertainers—women like Liv Tyler, daughter of Aerosmith front man Steven Tyler; Kate Hudson, daughter of actress Goldie Hawn and actor, comedian, and musician Bill Hudson; and Gwyneth Paltrow, daughter of actress Blythe Danner and writer/producer Bruce Paltrow.

But McCartney's own pedigree would cause its share of problems, and the designer would not have a smooth road throughout the ride of her career. She would have to fight the curse of her famous last name; a variety of people, including designer Karl Lagerfeld, would criticize her rise in the industry and her talent, saying that she only got where she is because of a certain Beatle father. In the end, McCartney would prove her critics wrong, showing that not only did she have talent, but she had staying power and the ability to build a brand worn by women around the globe.

1

A "Normal" Childhood

L inda Eastman was a rock photographer who had grown up in Scarsdale, New York. Married briefly while in college as a fine arts major, she had a young daughter named Heather. By the time her work was gaining recognition, she was a single mom out on the road doing shoots for big-time magazines such as *Life* and *Rolling Stone*, capturing images of heavy-hitting rockers like Jimi Hendrix, Janis Joplin, Bob Dylan, the Doors, the Grateful Dead, and the Mamas and the Papas. So it was really no surprise when she was asked to photograph the group that was most likely the biggest band in the world at the time, British superstars the Beatles. The shoot was for the release of their soon-to-be iconic record *Sergeant Pepper's Lonely Hearts Club Band*. This, however, turned out to be more than just a regular photo shoot. The Fab Four's much-adored singer, guitarist, and

Stella's difficult birth inspired Paul McCartney to call his new band "Wings." With Linda as a member, the band became a family affair as Stella and her siblings were brought along on tours. *Above,* Linda carries Stella while on tour with Wings in Helsinki, Finland.

songwriter Paul McCartney took note of the blonde photographer and was soon smitten. Very much in love, Linda and Paul married on March 12, 1969, with almost the whole world watching and hearts of women everywhere breaking as Paul McCartney, the boy from Liverpool, became a married man.

Family was an important concept almost immediately for Paul and Linda. Paul adopted Linda's daughter, Heather, who was six when they married. And soon after their nuptials, the famous couple began having children of their own. Daughter Mary was born in the summer of 1969. And on September 13, 1971, in London, not long after the breakup of the Beatles, the pair welcomed another special little bundle of joy into the world—Stella

Nina McCartney. The couple was especially grateful for little Stella because during the birth, Linda and her tiny baby nearly died. The ordeal had Paul praying that his child be born "on the wings of an angel." This situation and thought inspired Paul to name his new band with Linda "Wings." The newborn herself was named as homage to the two great-grandmothers on Linda's side of the family, both of whom were coincidentally named Stella.

FARMERS WHO ROCK

Home life for the McCartney girls seemed like anyone else's—for the most part. During most of the 1970s, the McCartney family lived in a large, white Georgian-style home located in London near Regent's Park. Paul now had his band Wings, and Linda took part playing keyboards and singing backup vocals. So whenever Mom and Dad hit the road for a tour, the children went along. For the McCartneys, sticking together as a family was important. At hotels after a show, the rock star parents would put their three daughters to bed—the two oldest into an actual bed, and little Stella into an improvised "crib" of a pulled-out dresser drawer made comfortable with pillow and blankets.

By the time Stella was 10, the family—which now included a baby boy named James born in 1977—had settled down on a farm far from the public eye in West Sussex, England, which lies on England's southern coast about 90 minutes away from the hustle and bustle of the city. There the family lived in a modest two-bedroom farmhouse shaped like a lantern and encircled by woods. The three girls shared one bedroom, and Paul and Linda the other. Baby James had sleeping quarters in the dining room. They lived a bucolic life, raising sheep and horses and growing organic vegetables.

A few years later, they moved to another farm only five minutes away, this one bigger, with two floors and five bedrooms, so that each child could have a room of his or her own. But the setting was the same: a simple life of land, farm dogs, chickens, cats, geese, and horses. The only thing that might have given away the fortune

ELEMENTS OF STYLE

I'm obviously hugely inspired by how my mum wore clothes, and my dad. But for me, it was more their attitudes. The way he would wear a bespoke suit and beard. The way she would wear a little YSL jacket with a straw vintage dress underneath. It was the attitude behind it, that I'm-going-to-do-it-my-way, I'm-allowed-to-do-this . . . mentality.

—*Stella McCartney, "Women in Luxury,"* Time, *September 4, 2008*

behind the simplicity were the paintings by Matisse and Magritte that hung casually on the walls. It was this upbringing of love for nature, land, and animals that would come to influence Stella so strongly later in life. Her country childhood proved to be an influence on her work. Today it can be seen in the things she takes from the country for inspiration: crystals, flowers, and nature itself.

Stella took easily to this natural setting and was a little tomboy who never owned a doll as a child. Instead, she reveled in riding horses, catching frogs, and exploring the woods. She also liked to make people laugh. Later, the tomboy quality would come out in her designs as well, adding a bit of masculinity to her feminine styles.

GROWING UP IN THE REAL WORLD

Paul and Linda had a strong desire for their children to know what life was like in the real world, not in the world of rock stardom and fame. They wanted Stella and her siblings to know that family and friends were what were truly important, not what money could buy. As a result, there were no nannies or bodyguards around, and the children all wore each other's hand-me-downs. The McCartney siblings all went to the local state school in East Sussex, where they were known for their good manners. And although Paul and Linda did employ an older woman for help with domestic chores,

Linda performed all the duties of a normal mom, picking the kids up from school, making them tea, and sending them off to bed after the family all watched the "telly" together. She also made their lunches. The strict vegetarian made some of these with a lunch meat substitute called Bolono—and the sandwiches were much

Determined to provide a normal life for their children, Linda and Paul moved their growing family into a big house in the country. There, Stella, her siblings, and her parents (*above*) played with animals and rode horses, away from the world of celebrity and rock and roll.

An Artistic Brood

Perhaps it is no surprise that the McCartney children each seemed to choose a path of an artistic nature. Mom was a photographer with several books to her name; Dad was a world-famous musician, not to mention a strong supporter of artists and their culture. Stella's half sister, Heather, is a pottery designer. Linda and Paul's firstborn, Mary, who can be seen as a child on the back cover of Paul's 1970 debut solo album in a photo taken by Linda, became a photographer in her own right—focusing on portrait and fashion. Younger brother, James, is a musician and sculptor.

coveted by the kids' school chums. Since Mom was from New York, summers were spent across the ocean on Long Island.

Paul had always recorded, whether in their London home or in an outbuilding on the farm, so Stella knew that her father was a popular musician. Young Stella, however, had little idea of the enormity of that celebrity. In 2007, on Exposay.com, Paul said, "There was this one morning where they were riding their little ponies in Scotland, and Stella said to me, 'Dad, you're Paul McCartney, aren't you?' and I said, 'Yes, darling, but I'm daddy really.'" Stella herself said that her father's true fame did not hit her until age 18 when she saw him performing in Rio de Janeiro in front of a crowd of 200,000 fervent fans.

Life, however, was not always normal, everyday living. When one has famous parents, they often have famous houseguests as well. Occasionally, other popular musicians like Stevie Wonder or Mick Jagger would come to call on the McCartney family. To the McCartney children, these people were not really celebrities, they were just their parents' friends. Paul and Linda made these visits

Despite the occasional celebrity houseguests, Stella's childhood was relatively normal. While she was able to reap the benefits of being a celebrity child, she also longed to distance herself from her parents and their achievements.

a learning experience for their children and taught them not to name-drop about famous houseguests with their chums at school.

Stella could not help but be a bit starstruck when it came to Michael Jackson, and she can still recall one particular disappointment in her young life involving the future king of pop. In a September 2001 *New Yorker* article, she said, "When I was about ten we were all going to go to a Jackson Five concert. All of us kids were upstairs in a back room beforehand, and I had a puff of a cigarette. When it was time to leave for the concert, I went to kiss my dad goodbye, and he smelled it and said, 'Stella, did you smoke a cigarette?' And I said, 'Noooo.' I was totally busted, and I didn't get to go to the concert."

For Stella, fame had its downside as well. She hated days when she missed the school bus and had to be driven in the family Mercedes—she did not want to call attention to herself. So when she began to get unwanted recognition as the famous daughter she was, she invented the name Stella Martin to disassociate herself from her celebrity parents. The famous McCartney name she was trying to escape would continue to haunt her later as she made her way into the world of fashion.

2

The Fashion-World Fledgling

The fashion bug hit Stella early in life, and she showed interest in clothing and fashion even as a child. When still quite young, she drew an entire clothing collection, and like many other future designers, was crafting and creating her own clothes by her early teens. Her first significant piece was a jacket she made from an artificial-suede upholstery fabric. At age 15, she became an apprentice to famous high-end French fashion designer Christian Lacroix, without any assistance from her parents. Stella was learning and starting from the very bottom. She did not even get to hold pins—her assignment was lace and shoe detail. During her short stint with Lacroix, she helped the team that put together his first official couture collection. Stella continued with other early learning experiences, which included helping British designer Betty Jackson, where Stella learned one of the rudiments of fashion—sewing buttonholes. She also had a summer internship in the fashion department of British *Vogue*.

GETTING SERIOUS

In 1992, McCartney's fascination with fashion led her to choose London's Central Saint Martins College of Art and Design, which has bred numerous high-profile designers. McCartney made this choice even though her mother tried to discourage her from a life in the fashion world—and the public eye. According to a March 2005 article in *The Independent*, Linda had warned her daughter by saying, "It's such a competitive, fickle world. Do you really want to do something where people judge you?"

Despite her mother's concerns, McCartney would not be held back and committed herself to a three-year bachelor degree in fashion design. In keeping with her parents' desire to give their children a normal life, she made her own way through college,

Looking for a more hands-on experience, McCartney supplemented her design college education with a job as a tailor's apprentice in a shop on Savile Row. Known for their traditional, high-quality tailoring, the men's clothing shops on Savile Row have dressed many important figures, including Winston Churchill, Prince Charles, and Napoleon III.

ELEMENTS OF STYLE

The first day [on Savile Row] . . . I started off by doing . . . the chest area. In a tailored suit, there are three fabrics that build up the chest area—horsehair and damask and canvas—and you sandwich them together with a stitch called a padding stitch. The padding starts below the shoulder and, on a man's jacket, it comes down below the chest. On a woman's jacket it stops higher. . . . Anyway, that's where they started me, and I learned a lot, and it was all very real. English tailoring is not fancy-schmancy—it's just, like, a suit. Nothing changes. It's like a house with two windows and a door—that's all there is. That makes it limiting in one way, but it's really concentrated and interesting at the same time. For example, almost everyone's got one shoulder that's higher than the other, and at that level of tailoring you compensate for it. Or if a man's got a pigeon chest you make him look as though he hasn't. Learning how to do all that takes years and years. Just learning how to put a sleeve on a jacket takes three years—it's the last thing an apprentice learns. Some of the most important things that I myself learned had to do with form and the body. . . . Another thing about Savile Row is that they really work only for men; they hardly ever make women's suits. So it was interesting to me to see how limited they were and to see how much room there was for me to . . . apply men's fabric to a woman's suit.

—Stella McCartney in "Going Solo" by David Owen, The New Yorker, *September 17, 2001*

working as a dishwasher at a local restaurant to pay her bills and buy the outfits she wanted to wear.

McCartney felt the school itself got high marks for its instruction on theory, but she felt it was lacking in its teaching about technique. So, partly inspired by her mom and the men's bespoke suits she liked to wear, the fashion student became an apprentice to a tailor, Edward Sexton, on Savile Row, known for its tradition

McCartney's efforts to earn her degree without the help of her famous parents were often met with skepticism and pettiness. Some of her classmates believed she had an unfair advantage and complained when McCartney received media attention for her designs.

of well-respected and long-standing clothing companies. At that time, such a decision was seen as a bit eccentric for a student of fashion. As David Owen's 2001 *New Yorker* article said, it was "like art students insisting on learning how to draw." Later, however, because of McCartney's and fellow designer Alexander McQueen's success (McQueen also apprenticed on Savile Row), learning the technical side of fashion by apprenticing on Savile Row became an almost mandatory part of education for students learning fashion design. As a tailor's apprentice, McCartney learned to hone her technical skill for the intricate art and, later, she would become well respected for her clothes' fine physical construction.

STICKS AND STONES

To her instructors, McCartney may have proved to be a focused and creative student of design, but her fellow students were not as easily impressed. Try as she might to be just another student, some classmates resented Stella's lineage and suspected that her name got her into the school, not her talent. McCartney herself says she was shy and that others may have interpreted her distance as being snobbish or stuck up. She thought everyone hated her, and possibly she had good reason to think so. Occasionally, she faced taunts and bullying. One incident happened just before her Central Saint Martins graduation show. Stella had some Scrabble letters that were going to be used within the show. Someone with a bit of malicious intent rearranged the letters to read "Daddy's Girl." The budding designer's choice to have her supermodel friends Naomi Campbell, Kate Moss, and Yasmin Le Bon, wife of Duran Duran lead singer Simon Le Bon, strut her designs down the catwalk did not sit well with other students, either. They saw it as an attempt to show off. But according to a March 2005 article from *The Independent*, McCartney reportedly said of her decision, "Other students ask their friends to model and I've asked mine."

None of this deterred McCartney, and the 1995 graduation show went on, albeit with a circuslike atmosphere. Sir Paul McCartney's little girl was graduating, and that got reporters' attention. They swarmed in for the somewhat star-studded event because with celebrity models and Mom and Pop McCartney in the front row, this would not be just any graduation show. McCartney used her

Design Central

Central Saint Martins is a design college of international acclaim and a prestigious history. It is the result of a 1989 merger of two schools. One was Central School of Arts and Crafts, which was founded in 1896 and known for its design and art programs, including theater and industrial and graphic design. The other was St. Martin's School of Art, founded in 1854 and known for its fashion and fine art programs.

During the years, the school's students have made great contributions to art and the world of fashion, not only in Britain, but around the globe. Graduates include renowned painters Lucien Freud (grandson of Sigmund Freud) and Frank Auerbach. In the realm of fashion, graduates have included John Galliano, Alexander McQueen, and Christopher Kane. Other alumni have gone on to work as designers or design directors for big labels such as Burberry, Calvin Klein, Chanel, Christian Dior, DKNY, Dolce & Gabbana, Donna Karan, Gucci, Jil Sander, Louis Vuitton, Marc Jacobs, Nina Ricci, Prada, and Versace.

The fashion program there is considered one of the most rigorous and respected in the world. In fact, it is the only college with a program so professional that it holds its own show for graduates' work each February in conjunction with London Fashion Week. The show is attended by buyers, editors, and prospective employers, each looking to spot the fashion world's top new talent.

McCartney undoubtedly had a lot of competition getting into the prestigious fashion college. The program is extremely competitive. In 2010, 1,500 applicants vied for 155 spots in the BA program and 500 vied for the 46 spots in the MA program. There is no wonder why. Of all the designers showing collections during London's Fashion Week in 2010, approximately half had attended Central Saint Martins.

father's tune "Stella May Day" as one of her runway songs. So as hard as she may have wanted to be like all of the other students, she obviously was not. Her graduation from Central Saint Martins made the papers. But again, other graduates were disgruntled. The swarm of

Savile Row specializes in making "bespoke suits"—made-to-order clothing designed for a specific client—and the pieces in McCartney's first collection were created in the same fashion. Although her work was well received, McCartney quickly learned that her clothes were too labor intensive to be mass-produced. *Above,* a partially finished bespoke suit.

photographers and reporters that had come to cover the event left promptly after McCartney's segment of the show was over.

"STELLA" TAKES OFF

All in all, the show was a smashing success. Although it does not happen with many graduation collections, McCartney's—which included a feminine version of those Savile Row suits—was bought by Tokio, a Japanese clothing retailer with stores in both Japan and London. The only trouble was that the up-and-coming designer had not created her collection with mass production in mind; in fact, she had sewn each of the pieces in her Notting Hill garage. In the now-famous words of *Project Runway*'s Tim Gunn, she quickly learned to "make it work," and with some substitutions, the clothes became more than one-offs.

Her designs were also licensed and sold by respectable retail giants like Bergdorf Goodman and Neiman Marcus in both the United Kingdom and the United States and could soon be seen on famous British beauties like actress Patsy Kensit. McCartney said she was forced to learn the business side of the industry fast—something her Central Saint Martins education had not taught her. One of the things that she was a little disappointed to find was that shops wanted outfits, something that went strictly against her McCartney mix-and-match methodology.

For the young designer, graduation was only the beginning. She opened her own boutique and took her feminine style of lace and romance and coupled it with the fine tailoring she had learned on Savile Row. Her designs at the time strongly favored slip dresses and flowing silk skirts. She produced the items in her own London apartment and called the line Stella. McCartney, however, was still a novice in some ways. She said she knew little of London Fashion Week, one of the biggest events in fashion held twice yearly by the British Fashion Council, and in her second year, she put on her own show for Fashion Week. She asked about 20 press people to join her at her small studio in Notting Hill. Attendees hung out on couches while three models sauntered around the room and chatted with the guests. It was amateur in comparison to the shows put on by well-known designers, and, looking back, McCartney herself called it "cute." McCartney's design life, however, was soon to hit the big time when an unexpected visitor stopped by her unpretentious little London boutique.

3

Reinvigorating Chloé

The name of the man who visited McCartney in December 1996 was Mounir Moufarrige, but the young designer did not know that at the time. Moufarrige simply introduced himself as a shop owner not unlike herself, only from Rome, Italy. He politely asked her a lengthy list of questions about her designs and her ideas and philosophies on how to sell clothing to women of various ages.

It was not until later that Moufarrige revealed his true identity as president of the long-standing French women's clothing label Chloé. Moufarrige was scouting for a new chief designer to lead his ailing 47-year-old company. Chloé had been at its peak in the 1970s when under the helm of Karl Lagerfeld; back then it thrived as a fashion house known for its delicate and whimsical clothing. But after Lagerfeld's departure in 1983, the ready-to-wear house

> ### ELEMENTS OF STYLE
>
> *I think my design philosophy is to make clothes that allow women to reflect their inner confidence and to help women have the confidence to be different and to be noticed, but in a very subtle, attractive kind of way. And it's a huge compliment when people fall for it. When I first started designing, a friend of mine bought one of my slip dresses, and she . . . got all these compliments. . . . And she was like, "The dress!" That, to me, is the ultimate. The goal is to keep it real, and not to insult the client, and to design clothes that people can really wear but that still get them noticed.*
>
> —Stella McCartney in "Going Solo" by David Owen,
> The New Yorker, *September 17, 2001*

lost its luster and never seemed to regain it—even after Lagerfeld's return in 1992. Moufarrige was hoping that an infusion of new blood would revive his suffering business and therefore took it upon himself to interview 41 different designers for the position as director of the House of Chloé. McCartney and her views on women's wear and the business of selling to the female market had impressed Moufarrige tremendously. He told the *New York Times* in April 1997 that "Stella has a strong character, and over all she really understands feminine clothes and real clothes for real women, which are needed right now."

A NEW CREATIVE DIRECTION

After six months of talks, McCartney—at the young age of 25, and with only two collections under her belt—was offered the job as the Parisian house's creative director. The move was a boon to her career. In the *New Yorker* in 2001, she said that after her small and simple London fashion show, she had begun to realize that she could not keep going by herself. "My business was growing so fast that it was starting to get away from me. It was just me and two part-time helpers, and we couldn't keep up. That was why I said yes to Chloé. I thought, This will take the pressure off everything in London. I will just slip away and go to Paris for a while, and nobody will even notice." McCartney could not have been more wrong about the attention her appointment—and her name—would garner. The new head of Chloé was the talk of the town, and not all of the chatter was positive.

Many in the fashion world bristled at the selection of a designer so young and with so little real-world experience to lead an established house of fashion. McCartney was an unknown quantity—she had been out of fashion school for only 20 months. Her critics included the exiting Lagerfeld, who, according to Hellomagazine.com, famously said, "Chloé should have taken a big name. They did, but in music, not fashion. Let's hope she's as gifted as her father."

By April 1997, McCartney was getting ready to put her own collection on hold; she would fill spring orders for clients like Neiman Marcus and Bergdorf Goodman, but then her talent would be devoted strictly to her new employer, Chloé. She moved to Paris and was the official head of the French ready-to-wear house, whose headquarters are located at Rue du Faubourg St. Honoré. Reportedly, her salary was a hefty one million francs (about $177,000 at the time) each year.

A FINE START

The first Chloé show—for the spring-summer 1998 collection—took place in the fall of 1997, and with it, the newly appointed chief of design put many of her critics to rest. The collection—highlighted by items like lacy petticoat skirts in combination with other pieces that showed off McCartney's fine tailoring skill—was very well received. The looks were an up-to-date version of the delicate, floating, and feminine 1970s fashions that her mother had adored.

Some industry reporters did point out that the collection was neither bold nor groundbreaking, but it was lauded for its clean

Many in the fashion industry were skeptical when McCartney was appointed creative director of Chloé. In spite of the criticism, McCartney's work reinvigorated the French label and inspired other designers to soften the style of their own collections. *Above,* Paul and Linda attend their daughter's Chloé fashion show; Linda died a month after this photo was taken.

lines and delicate and sexy feel—the kind of clothing that had wide appeal to consumers. In fact, the romantic look of the new Chloé fashions soon became a strong influence on other designers, and it was not long before the plainer styles of the earlier 1990s were being replaced with softer, fresher looks. McCartney had inspired a subtle fashion revolution.

The accolades were a welcome change for the French label. Chloé had been doing so poorly in recent years that the last two shows had actually been booed off the runway. Under McCartney's leadership, sales soon saw a significant boost.

Until this time, Chloé's clientele consisted mainly of middle-aged women, but this would soon change. McCartney took a risk. She chose to follow her own instinct and make designs that appealed to her, reinventing Chloé as a line that was both a little funky and slightly sexy. In a later *Newsweek* article by Veronica Chambers, McCartney said this of her approach to the position: "I didn't think of the old Chloé customer [when I started]; the minute you stop and think, 'Will this suit a 50-year-old woman?' you lose your design instinct. I think about what I want to wear and what my friends want to wear." Apparently, McCartney's instincts were just what a lot of women wanted.

THE LOSS OF LINDA

In 1998, McCartney's soaring career meant little when her family suffered a great blow. Beloved McCartney family matriarch, Linda, lost her three-year battle with breast cancer. She had been diagnosed with the disease in 1995 and had undergone surgery as well as numerous chemotherapy sessions. Although the treatments extended her life, the cancer eventually spread to her liver.

Shortly before her death, Linda did make it to her daughter's Chloé show on March 11 in Paris, happily watching her child's success and enjoying the reward of her hard work while sitting between husband, Paul, and son, James. Only a month later, Linda would be gone.

During Linda's final days, the family all gathered at Paul and Linda's Arizona ranch to spend time together. She passed away surrounded by her loved ones on April 17. At the time, the McCartneys released a statement that Linda had died in Santa Barbara, California, in order to put the media off the scent and gain the famous family a bit of time to grieve in peace. Memorial services were held in England, California, and New York.

Stella McCartney, however, did not lose herself in this tragedy. She kept focused and just kept going—her work was her fuel. In a 2002 interview with *Harper's Bazaar*, the profound effect of Linda's death on her famous designer daughter was evident when, in a rare moment of personal revelation, McCartney briefly discussed her mother's death: "Obviously my life has changed a great deal. It changed the moment my mum was diagnosed with breast cancer, and I still haven't really come to terms with it, to be honest. It's the worst thing that could ever have happened to me and my family. It's amazing how things change; I mean, you could never imagine."

CHLOÉ TRANSFORMS

By 1999, when McCartney had been chief designer of the French fashion house for two years, sales were $421.4 million and the product was selling well in stores like Neiman Marcus, Bergdorf's, and Saks Fifth Avenue, whose president, Phillip Miller, commented in a 1999 *Newsweek* article that the rising star's design direction was "fashion that can sell to a lot of people." Chloé now had a new, younger audience eager for McCartney's hip and trendy styles. Part of the *The Washington Post*'s comments about McCartney's instinct for design included this glowing remark: "Chloé has not just gotten substantially better. It has been transformed."

Encouraged by the newfound success of the line, Chloé opened its first new store in 20 years in Manhattan. Demand for Chloé was at an all-time high. Part of the proof could be found at the new boutique in New York, where a pair of McCartney's stylish aviator sunglasses, priced at almost $200, had a waiting list of 150 people.

McCartney, however, still had her detractors. People like British fashion editor Jeff Banks took their shots at the famous-named designer; *The Independent* quoted him as saying McCartney was "just an amateur who has made it in the fashion world on the back of her dad's money."

Perhaps still stinging from her mother's death only a year before, McCartney finally flung back and uttered to a reporter what may be her most famous quote, reprinted in a 2005 article for *The Independent*:"When I would make a good drawing in primary school, it was because my dad was famous. Or if I got a part in a school play, it was because Dad was a Beatle. What do I do? Do I become a smackhead and live off my parents' fortune?" And McCartney had a point. So many children of celebrities become known for their partying and run-ins with the law—the McCartney children in general were shining exceptions—due in large part to the way they were raised by Paul and Linda.

As children of famous rock stars, McCartney and her friend, actress Liv Tyler (*left*), have established careers for themselves based on their talents and have avoided major scandal. McCartney's work with Chloé impressed most of those in the fashion industry, but there were people who still attributed her success to having a famous father.

RUMORS START TO SPREAD

McCartney went a little edgier with the Chloé style in the label's Paris fashion show in October 1999. The designer seemed to be returning to her fashion school roots by having models jaunt down the catwalk in skimpy short shorts; chain tops; dark, tight-fitting jeans; flirty suits; and embroidered shirts with a slightly hippie look. One fashion reporter commented that such clothes might prove harder to sell since they were not as easily wearable as those in earlier Chloé collections.

The show was notable in more than just its departure from the imminently wearable and breezy Chloé fashions of previous shows. In the fall of 1999, rumors started to swirl among fashion's top editors and industry insiders that Chloé's golden girl might defect from the French house to lead Italian label Gucci. Speculation had it that Tom Ford, Gucci's head, might be making a move due to Gucci's recent acquisition of Yves Saint Laurent. Insiders believed that Ford would be promoted to creative director, overseeing both houses, Gucci and Yves Saint Laurent, while McCartney would be tapped as Ford's successor at Gucci. So rumors were especially fueled by Tom Ford's seat at the side of Sir Paul McCartney during the Paris show.

Some people, however, were convinced that a Gucci-McCartney deal would never go through. Her sexy designs were no problem; they would fit right in at the house of Gucci, if in fact, Ford was trying to sway the young creative director. But it seemed almost a certainty that working for Gucci would mean working with leather, and McCartney would never go for that, given her vegetarian and animal-rights stance. That October, Chloé president Ralph Toledano tried to put the rumors to bed and stated in a *Newsweek* article that no move was imminent: "They said she would be gone by the end of September. Where is she? Downstairs, designing clothes." In a December 1999 *New York Times* article, McCartney herself would not talk specifics about her job situation, but she did mention that after meeting at a party thrown by Madonna, she and Ford had casually chatted about possible prospects with the Italian label. Speculation, however, for the most part, ended when McCartney signed another contract, keeping her attached to Chloé.

As McCartney continued to find success with Chloé, many people began to wonder if she would move to another fashion label. Rumors of secret talks with Gucci were reported in the media, but McCartney stayed with the French company until 2001. *Above,* McCartney greets the audience at the end of a 1999 Chloé fashion show in Washington, D.C.

CHLOÉ 2001

McCartney had proved the skeptics wrong. She was the fashion industry's rising star, taking risks and turning profits. In 2001, McCartney took a gamble by taking Chloé in yet another new direction. She developed a line called See, which had a more casual look and a lower price point. Overall, sales during the course of her tenure at Chloé went up an astonishing 500 percent.

Dressing the Material Girl

When music icon Madonna announced that she would be marrying British director Guy Ritchie, the press went wild. McCartney would have a pivotal role at the auspicious occasion. The December 22, 2000, ceremony took place at the foot of the staircase in the Great Hall of a Scottish castle. Surrounded by hundreds of lit candles, Madonna's four-year-old daughter, Lourdes, lead the procession, throwing rose petals from a basket as she descended the stairs. Madonna followed in a gown designed by McCartney, her friend and maid of honor. The dress made of ivory-colored silk was a breathtaking strapless number with a fitted corset bodice and long, cascading train. To complete her wedding day look, Madonna wore an antique veil, a pair of Jimmy Choo shoes, and a diamond tiara on loan from a London jeweler. Perhaps the true shining crown, however, was the 37-carat, 2 ½-inch (6-centimeter) diamond cross draped around her neck—a custom piece made exclusively for the Material Girl from the House of Harry Winston in New York.

The groom was dressed in a teal blazer and a plaid Scottish kilt of navy and green. He also wore a pair of antique diamond cuff links—a wedding gift from Madonna. Ritchie and Madonna's four-month-old son, Rocco, wore a kilt matching that of his father's. Lourdes's own long, ivory dress was a McCartney original as well.

The understated yet stylish maid of honor wore a gray and beige pants ensemble of her own design.

In a 2001 *New Yorker* article, revered (and feared) *Vogue* editor in chief Anna Wintour summed up McCartney's turnaround of the Chloé label: "What Stella did was to surprise everybody, by very, very quickly developing her own style. It's very much the way she dresses herself, and you can feel her in all the collections she does. We have so few women designers who are really important in the field of fashion, and it's great to have someone like Stella joining the ranks. She has made a lot of very young, very attractive girls want to buy those clothes."

The French house benefited immensely and continued to go strong with McCartney at the helm; clothes of the once-tired fashion label could be seen on the likes of Hollywood's hottest actresses—Kate Hudson, Nicole Kidman, and Cameron Diaz to name a few. Madonna even sported a pair of Chloé trousers in her "Ray of Light" video.

The collection that McCartney put together for Chloé in spring 2001 had its Paris debut at the famous Louvre Museum. Attendees, including the designer's dad, Liv Tyler, singer Chrissie Hynde, and British billionaire Richard Branson, sat on fancy chairs in one of the museum's elegant galleries. Models showed off fake-fur coats with embroidery that from a distance made the coats look as if they had been splashed with gold. *Guardian* writer Jess Cartner Morley called the event "an elegant, sure-footed show, full of gentle wit and lovingly crafted, detailed clothes." The show would be McCartney's last for Chloé.

4

Gucci's New Girl

Perhaps there had been some truth to those rumors floating around in 1999, because McCartney was swayed by Gucci head Tom Ford to join the group in April 2001 under her own signature label. Such a deal meant the animal-rights designer would not only control the designs, she would also be in charge of what materials were used, so if she did not want to use leather or fur, she would not have to. Some people, however, thought that McCartney had sold out by going to Gucci. One of those people was Karl Lagerfeld, who called her ideals "grotesque" and whom a 2005 article from *The Independent* quoted as saying, "Everyone knows Gucci has made millions of dollars working with leather. When she signed with them, she closed the chapter as far as holding these sorts of scruples with any kind of credibility."

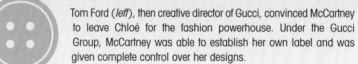

Tom Ford (*left*), then creative director of Gucci, convinced McCartney to leave Chloé for the fashion powerhouse. Under the Gucci Group, McCartney was able to establish her own label and was given complete control over her designs.

McCartney frankly did not care what people like Lagerfeld thought. Not to mention, she had a plan in mind. The activist designer hoped eventually to become an educator within the industry, teaching designers at other houses about alternative choices to materials made from animal products and encouraging their use.

With humor, Gucci president and CEO Domenico de Sole called the negotiations with McCartney the toughest ever— apparently, she was not known in the industry as Stella Steel for nothing. The Gucci Group bought 50.1 percent of Stella McCartney for a whopping £6 million (about $8.6 million at the time). Starting a signature label under the Gucci empire had its benefits. Not only would McCartney have Gucci funds backing her endeavor, she would have access to the company's extensive production workshops, factories, and marketing capabilities.

On an early visit to one such factory in Italy, the new Gucci member made more than a good impression. One company executive said, "everyone liked her." He also commented on her effective and congenial way of working with a team. To get the label off the ground, McCartney created a team of her own, and a rather international one at that. She surrounded herself with four design assistants—one from South Korea, one from Israel, one from Germany, and one whose mother came from Cameroon. Three of the four were graduates of her alma mater, Central Saint Martins.

The move put McCartney in the spotlight, and she started getting attention in other ways, too. Although she has always had celebrity parents and famous friends, she soon realized that she was becoming a bit of a celebrity in her own right. In early August 2001, a report surfaced in the *New York Post* about the designer and a supposed date with the publisher of British interior-design magazine *Wallpaper*. She and the man in question, Alasdhair Willis, had been seen in an unmistakably romantic act outside a pub in London. Seeing herself as the main subject in the gossip pages of a newspaper was a new experience for McCartney and one that she found took some getting used to.

THE START OF STELLA McCARTNEY LTD.

The move to Gucci meant McCartney had a lot to do and little time to do it—her first collection would need completion quickly for a fall debut only a few months later. Not only did she have to find staff, like her four assistants, and suppliers, she had to relocate back to London from Paris—basically, she had to reorganize her entire life.

One of the most crucial things that had to be done was to create a logo for the new Stella McCartney brand, no easy feat since a brand logo must encompass many aspects of a label in one fairly simple design. A September 2001 *New Yorker* article titled "Going Solo" captured McCartney's well-contemplated logo design thoughts as she spoke to a young graphic artist:

> I want my logo to be timeless and tasteful and slick and charming and individual and vintage-y and not really over-the-top industrial, and I want it to have some little element that's cool. I'm not really a huge fan of curvy. I think it would be nice to take an old font, something very beautiful and amazing, and then make it new and modern. I know I have to live with this. It has to be something that will work on labels and bags and storefronts and everything else, and it has to make sense in different cultures, and it can't be too feminine, because I may want to do men's clothes someday.
>
> I like the idea of working my initials in somehow—S.N.M., Stella Nina McCartney. I like the fact that there are two "C"s together in my name, a big "C" and a small "c." There are certain colors that I like. I've thought about putting a horse in there, because I'm mad about horses. And my name means "star," although that's not my favorite image. I shouldn't even tell you these things, because I don't want you to come back to me with a lot of stars or a lot of horses. The logo just has to echo me. The whole thing about my line is mixing and matching, not dictating to people, not being oppressive.

THE ROLLER COASTER BEGINS

Almost immediately, McCartney knew that she wanted her label to be differentiated from the collections she had designed for Chloé. She wanted her namesake label to represent her—the things she likes, and the way she likes to dress. Unfortunately, the move got off to a rocky start for McCartney when her first collection under the Stella McCartney name debuted in Paris in October, only a few months after signing the deal. She moved away from the flirty, feminine, and flowing garments that had made Chloé so wildly successful and transitioned her design aesthetic to something a bit edgier, like suits with the phrase "trouble and strife" emblazoned down the side. McCartney herself noted the change, stating that Stella was all about minimal that season.

The acclaim was minimal as well, with most of the reviews less than flattering. The 9/11 tragedy in New York had happened only the month before, and troops were currently rushing into Afghanistan. Perhaps partially due to the timing and McCartney's choice of a loud laser show as part of the presentation, the show did not go over well. The whole event may have seemed overly politicized; at one point, the song "Give Peace a Chance" played overhead while models sauntered down the runway flashing the peace sign.

According to the Encyclopedia of World Biography, reporter Lisa Armstrong of New York Metro.com had this to say: "McCartney, who'd become a reliable source of lovely, easy on the eye garments, chose this moment to replace her stock-in-trade flirtiness with something more hard core." A description by yet another fashion reporter called the clothes "trashy and vulgar."

The result of such poor reviews was devastating, with some orders for the collection actually canceled. McCartney, however, showed her strength and humility as a leader. The next day, she apologized to all of her employees and went to see boss Tom Ford to talk about what had happened.

In all, the experience garnered her further criticism of being famous in the world of fashion only for her name. Truthfully, the name has its benefits. Rumor had it that McCartney wanted to call her line with the Gucci Group simply "Stella," like her first collections out of college. But the powers that be at Gucci insisted a joint venture could be made only if she were to use that famous last name in the label's title.

The criticisms hit McCartney hard. In the 2002 *New York* magazine article "Stella Nova," McCartney said, "I was really freaked out. People think I'm strong, but actually I wanted to crawl away. I thought, *I'm going to live in the country with my horse and I'll get a nine-to-five—I don't need this.*"

Her second collection, however, fared much better and aligned more closely to the style McCartney originally became known for—the pieces were young and fun with a bit of masculinity and a lot of fine tailoring.

A WEDDING BRINGS TROUBLE

On June 11, 2002, McCartney's father, Paul, married his girlfriend of two years, Heather Mills. The $3 million wedding and celebration, attended by rock veterans like Ringo Starr, Eric Clapton, and Sting, was held in Ireland. The celebration was not a happy one for all involved. Stella and her sister Mary were wary about Mills's intentions—at the time the couple met, Paul was 60 and Mills was 34, a 26-year-age difference. Although Paul and his bride to be met at a charity dinner, McCartney and her sister, not to mention much of the press, eyed Mills as a gold digger out to stake a claim on Sir Paul's millions and cause upset between the music legend and his beloved children.

According to reports, the animosity was subtle, but evident on the big day. Mary and Stella, who apparently encouraged her father to secure a prenuptial agreement, said not a word to Mills all day. During the family portrait session, the two sisters gabbed just as the photo shutter snapped. They left the festivities three hours

McCartney's first collection under her own name was a dramatic departure from her work at Chloé. Feminized suit jackets and flirty dresses were replaced with minimalistic suits with words written on them. The collection's poor reception compelled McCartney to return to a subtler look with her next collection. *Above,* Paul McCartney and his then girlfriend Heather Mills attend the Stella McCartney fashion show in 2001.

early—a bit of a snub to their father's new wife. A factor that may have set off the sister pair was Paul's decision not to wear his turquoise wedding ring from Linda that he had not taken off since her death four years earlier.

A Mother's Influence

Stella McCartney mentions frequently the influence that her mother, whom she considers a fashion icon, had on her own sense of style. She admired that Linda was more natural than polished and that she chose to wear clothes she liked rather than remain a slave to styles and trends. Her mother mixed vintage and modern, something McCartney does consistently in her collections. She said this of her mom's mix-and-match style in a 2001 *New Yorker* article by David Owen: "I remember going into her wardrobe when I was a little girl. She had some old Yves Saint Laurent dresses, because she and my dad had gone to some Paris couture shops when they first met, when they were young, but then right next to them were all the juxtapositions—an old vintage thirties dress, then a pair of platform boots, then a T-shirt, then a pair of . . . jeans. That kind of mixture pretty much became my philosophy."

And in the 2002 *New York* magazine article "Stella Nova," McCartney once again stresses her mother's effect on her, "My mum was a huge influence. The true fearlessness in the way she held herself, in life and in every way. To me, it's the most modern way to be a woman—a very real kind of femininity."

Linda's influence on her daughter and Stella's love for her mother remain evident; the designer dedicates a great many of her collections to Linda. In a 2002 *Harper's Bazaar* article, McCartney speaks to the reporter on the phone from her home and says, "I'm here looking at a picture that my mum took of Neil Young in the '60s. If you want to know something that inspires me, that inspires me." For McCartney, that quote probably says it all.

The bad feelings may have been justified for another reason as well. Stella was seemingly snubbed herself when it came to the bride's wedding dress. According to talk, Mills considered Stella's designs a bit "tarty" and nowhere near sophisticated enough for the occasion. Instead, Mills insisted in reports that she had designed her own $15,000 gown. The two British designers, however, who helped with the gown's creation felt snubbed as well. They said that Mills gave only vague guidance and that she took all the credit for their resulting five months of hard work.

The apparent bad feelings continued through the McCartney-Mills marriage until the pair finally separated in 2006. An ugly divorce followed, with Mills making a variety of terrible accusations against Paul. In the end, Stella and Mary were vindicated when Mills came across horribly—in both the proceedings and the public eye—with even the judge's ruling, according to the biography *Paul McCartney: A Life*, declaring the Beatles singer's ex as "erratic, out of control and vengeful." Perhaps the only good thing to come of the several-year union was daughter Beatrice, born in 2003.

LOOK OUT NEW YORK

The year 2002 proved to be a dramatic one for McCartney in other ways, as well. In September, it saw the opening of her flagship Stella McCartney store in, a bit ironically, New York's meatpacking district at 429 West Fourteenth Street. In fact, the stalwart vegetarian's store is situated in what was once Frank's Steakhouse and Maggio Beef. Indeed, one storefront on her block still proclaims that it has been in "Quality Meats" since 1903, and if one takes a turn around the corner, he or she will find Dave's Quality Veal. The choice of location is just one contradiction for a woman known for contradictions. She rails against being known for her famous name rather than her stylish designs, yet did not flinch from using Beatles music in her early shows for Chloé. She prefers staying close to home, riding horses in the countryside—yet has no qualms about being seen going out on the town with Gwyneth

Paltrow or Liv Tyler. Her career is based on dressing the rich and famous, yet she herself is the first to admit to being a bit of a slob and hardly ever dressing up or wearing makeup or jewelry.

McCartney insisted, however, that this increasingly chic area of New York, where former warehouses were being turned into nightclubs, boutiques, trendy restaurants, and art galleries, was better suited to her brand's style than, say, the more well-known fashion areas of New York like SoHo or Madison Avenue—the former of which McCartney felt was overrun with designers' shops to the point of being claustrophobic. In an interview with Adrian Michaels of FT.com, she said, "I looked at millions of other places, the usual suspects. They just weren't right. My kind of shop is expected to be a little bit different, a little bit fresher and a bit off the beaten track. I'm sure other areas are not losing anything, but you've got to create new things, haven't you? You've got to try to push it." The designer would not be the first to join the meatpacking district's changing landscape. Fellow Central Saint Martins alum Alexander McQueen also had a shop in the area.

Only about 18 months after venturing out to start her own company, the 31-year-old designer was excited but also terrified at the prospect of opening her own 4,000-square-foot (371.6-square-meter) store, which she was starting with the backing of Gucci Group money. To create a store that represented the Stella McCartney brand, the designer chose British architectural firm Universal Design Studio. Because McCartney is the creative mind behind her label, when it comes to her business, she controls anything needing artistic input. Therefore, she had a lot to do with the shop's design. She left the business side of the venture to her new American chief executive, James Seuss—a direct descendant of Theodore Seuss Geisel, also known as Dr. Seuss. Seuss came with an excellent CEO pedigree, having spent 12 years at Tiffany & Co. He landed the job after helping McCartney—an acquaintance of his for several years— through the rigorous negotiation process with Gucci. The match of creative and business minds seemed to be a good one. Seuss said the

In 2002, McCartney opened her flagship store in New York City's meatpacking district. Known for its slaughterhouses, the area has been transformed into one of the trendiest neighborhoods in the world. Other famous designers, such as Diane von Furstenburg and Christian Louboutin, also have opened stores near McCartney's flagship.

two had similar thoughts on growing the business and planned to take their time, moving not necessarily quickly, but calculatingly.

The store's interior is spare and modern while still maintaining a bit of whimsy. It was designed to be airy, open, and inviting—a safe haven in the wilds of the city. McCartney found the store's description in the official literature both a bit too fancy and a bit funny; it described the interior design concept in these terms: "abstract landscape as an antidote to the urban condition."

In an interview for *New York* magazine before the store's opening, the designer said that it would have been easy for her to do a pretty shop with a chandelier and a vintage upholstered chair. Instead, she wanted to do something more interesting, something that would be more forward thinking. McCartney's favorite feature of this labor of love was the dressing rooms—one of which was crafted by hand in Wales and paneled in inlaid wood in a design of tropical flowers and hummingbirds. The other dressing room was equally as elegant, upholstered in a hand-printed fabric with beads, faux gemstones, and antique Valentines attached.

Even though opening a store in New York only one year after 9/11 might have been a little risky, McCartney felt comfortable opening the first store in the Big Apple rather than London since she spent a lot of time on Long Island as a kid. The British design ingenue intended to stay positive about the store's prospects and hoped that its presence would help boost the city, even if in only a small way. She told FT.com before the store's opening, "I have no idea if New Yorkers will take to my style. I hope so. The research I do is from the heart. I try to create something that I would like and which reflects my personality. You're entering a dangerous area when you try to make things for people because you think that's what they want. You do it because you have a love for it. I'm creating stuff for me and my friends."

One thing McCartney was grateful for during the shop's opening weekend was her father's absence due to touring commitments. She was relieved that he would not be appearing in all the publicity pictures sure to hit the newspapers. Again, McCartney wanted to be recognized for her work, not her father's fame.

KEEPING BUSY

The store's opening was well timed since the designer's third Stella McCartney collection would be debuting the following month in Paris. In September, *Harper's Bazaar* carried a feature on McCartney that focused on the production of this third collection. She talked about the pressure she was under to get this collection right. Because of her name recognition and career success thus far, people were treating her as a fashion industry veteran when really this was only her third collection under the Gucci Group umbrella.

At the time, McCartney was in her least favorite part of the process of creating a new collection—the first fittings, something she referred to as "intense." She was also in the midst of creating costumes for friend Gwyneth Paltrow's upcoming film with Jude Law and Angelina Jolie, *Sky Captain and the World of Tomorrow.*

All in all, life was extremely busy for the fashion star; in *Harper's Bazaar,* one of her assistants described McCartney's average day as "manic"—the kind of day where the designer rarely stopped for the luxury of eating lunch. For a while, McCartney did yoga every day, but by now she felt too busy even for that. Sometimes she could not find time for breakfast, not even in the form of a smoothie.

Even as frenetic as her work life was, McCartney's personal life seemed healthy. She had been seeing Alasdhair Willis for about a year, and part of what she liked about him was that he understood her crazy schedule. Regardless of her own growing fame, she was also still living the kind of life that had been instilled in her by Paul and Linda. One might expect her to live in the most well-to-do section of London, as many with her level of fame and success would do, but she did not. Life for the most part was work, work, work. To relax, she would go back to her family home in East Sussex and ride her horse—one of her very favorite things to do.

Business just kept on rolling into 2003, and in May of that year, McCartney opened her second store—this one in Mayfair, London. To mark its opening, a large party was held with a variety of famous artists and actresses, including friend Madonna, to help celebrate the occasion.

McCartney also took time in August to design a T-shirt for a cause close to her heart—fighting breast cancer. Saks Fifth Avenue was involved in a Key to the Cure initiative, the proceeds from which would go to more than 60 organizations dedicated to women's cancer research. For her part, McCartney created a unique design on a white Danskin three-quarter-sleeve T-shirt that actress Nicole Kidman wore in advertisements for the cause. The price was a reasonable $30, and demand was high. Only 12,000 of the limited edition shirt were created, and before its release, the Saks Web site had a waiting list of more than 1,000 eager people.

5

Success in
Work, Life, and Love

On August 30, 2003, McCartney's personal life reached a new high as well when she married boyfriend and magazine publisher Alasdhair Willis. McCartney was obviously ecstatic and content at this moment in her life—a later 2007 article from *Elle* magazine quoted her as saying at the time, "I've never felt like this in a relationship before . . . it's just a dream." In her usual care-for-the-environment manner, McCartney and her husband to be asked that instead of gifts, guests offer trees for the newlyweds to plant on their country estate.

Held on the Scottish island of Bute, the happy event was definitely one of the social affairs of the season. Media, of course, desperately wanted to cover the ceremony, given the celebrity guest list, but Sir Paul managed to keep things quiet and in control by employing a team of 40 security personnel. The designer bride's

61-year-old father and his wife, Heather, now seven months pregnant, as well as about 140 guests, including Madonna, Liv Tyler, Kate Moss, actor Pierce Brosnan, and bridesmaid Gwyneth Paltrow, joined the happy couple on the 300-acre (121-hectare) estate of Mount Stuart, not far from the family farm. The location, featuring an impressive Victorian Gothic, was the home of the seventh Marquess of Bute.

Guests were brought to the estate's white marble chapel by way of horse-drawn carriages led by Clydesdales. McCartney, once again inspired by her mother, stood before the crowd wearing an updated version of the gown Linda had worn on her own wedding day with Paul. The Protestant ceremony lasted 20 minutes.

At the reception, guests enjoyed vegetarian fare like wild mushroom pie and vegetarian sausages, as well as the bagpipe music of the Campbeltown Pipe Band that had played on Paul's 1977 song "Mull of Kintyre." In all, the wedding—paid for by poppa Paul— with its three trucks of white English Beauty roses imported from Holland and a 10-minute fireworks display, cost about $2 million. To thank her father for the lovely and memorable day, Stella sent him a note and an expensive case of 1996 Burgundy wine.

STELLA BRANCHES OUT

Following her wedding, 32-year-old McCartney made another important business move; she launched her self-titled fragrance, a soft, feminine rose scent with hints of amber. The romantic perfume was packaged in a vintage-inspired, amethyst crystal bottle. The hip designer was now a fragrance entrepreneur as well.

McCartney did not stop the momentum. In October, she saw to the opening of her third store, this one strategically located in West Hollywood, California, a place where the designer's tailored yet slightly hard, deconstructed clothing would fit right in. Unlike New York's redesigned meatpacking location, this Stella

ELEMENTS OF STYLE

The biggest inspiration for the perfume—and my own personal goal—was to create a perfume that I would want to wear. I have a clear view of what I like and what I don't like. I wanted a smell that reflected my English side, something very traditional. At the same time I wanted to take my favourite smells and put them together in the same way that I use opposites and contradictions in my fashion design. And so the concept for the perfume was to try and create something pure and uncomplicated. I wanted a smell that was delicate, feminine—rose—mixed with a sexier and darker edge—amber. That's how I came up with those two facets. . . . I really wanted to create something precious. Not only is it a beautiful scent, but it is a stunning object to be cherished. It's one of the most expensive perfume bottles to make. . . . The perfume is based on a rose. I gave the perfumer an old picture of a rose. Imagine the most beautiful flower that is just on its way out, the flower head so heavy and its petals so loose that if you touch it, it collapses. I wanted to capture that beauty and fragility. That moment of perfection.

—Stella McCartney, http://www.escentual.com

McCartney is housed in a two-story former antique shop with an ivy-covered facade.

Of course, the store's launch meant another star-studded gathering. The Sunday evening extravaganza definitely had flair. Vegetarian wieners were served from hot dog carts, and fun house mirrors were placed for attendees like legendary music producer Quincy Jones, Oscar-winning actress and fellow Brit Cate Blanchett, and sisters Hilary and Haylie Duff to view themselves in. Other Stella enthusiasts in attendance were actress Debi Mazar, outfitted in a sea foam green ensemble that could also be found in the storefront window—with a price tag of $1,065. Actor Dylan McDermott's wife, Shiva Rose, arrived in clothes à la Stella as well, including a red slip and

French blue stockings. Actress Pamela Anderson was there, though not wearing Stella, explaining that she had worn Stella's designs each day not long ago while hosting London's Fashion Week. Portia de Rossi, another actress, wore a piece from McCartney's latest collection, a white fencing jacket. She called McCartney a really cool chick and continued to share more on her enthusiasm for the designer by telling a *New York Times* reporter, "It's great that there's a woman designing for 30-year-old women. When she first started designing for Chloé, I practically went bankrupt."

McCartney herself, admittedly known for dressing down more than for dressing up, had her hair pulled back into a ponytail and wore ruched pants that fell just below the knee and a black suit jacket from her own line.

The store's brick valet lot was turned into an English garden party for this opening night, complete with a stage and furniture in beige linen for guests to lounge comfortably. Old-fashioned cigarette girls with velvet-lined boxes meandered through the crowd, offering perfume samples, English candies, and Hollywood-brand gum to anyone who asked. As the sun began to set and the DJ began playing an energizing mix of classic disco tunes and current dance hits, the party really started to get going. By now more guests had arrived, including hot Hollywood couple Ashton Kutcher and Stella-clad Demi Moore, who turned heads immediately but quickly made their way to a sofa in the back of the garden. There were a flock of musicians as well: rapper Eve, Red Hot Chili Peppers' Anthony Kiedis, several former members of Guns N' Roses, and Rufus Wainwright to name a few.

Now guests could help themselves to cotton candy, taffy apples, sugared popcorn, and even classic English scones served with clotted cream. McCartney herself drank a special cocktail of the evening, a "Stellapolitan," and feasted on a veggie burger. The iconic 1951 movie *A Streetcar Named Desire* with a character named Stella played silently in the background. Silently, that is, until the famous Marlon Brando movie moment in which he yells with anguish,

"Stella! Stel-la!" At that point, throngs of people in the party crowd sounded Brando's words for him, shouting the name of their host.

A *New York Times* reporter caught McCartney in a moment powdering her nose with a friend's Chanel compact. He asked her what was next after this step in her career. "World domination," McCartney joked back. With three stores under her belt, McCartney's career itself was definitely no joke. The reporter's article appeared only a day or two later; however, given McCartney's distaste for references that link her career success to her father's name and celebrity, she may not have appreciated the article's title: "Sir Paul's Little Girl Opens in Los Angeles."

GOOD NEWS AND BAD NEWS

The year 2003 was good in so many ways for McCartney; not only had she married and opened her third Stella McCartney store, but she was also honored for her efforts against cancer. At the Unforgettable Evening event in Los Angeles, she was presented with the Woman of Courage Award. Given her late mother's own breast cancer experience, McCartney was undoubtedly proud of this important recognition.

The end of 2003 proved a bit of a hiccup in the McCartney momentum. Speculation was rising that McCartney's line might be cut from the Gucci Group of labels, especially since her cheerleader, Tom Ford, as well as current CEO, Domenico de Sole, had previously announced they'd be leaving the Italian clothing company, in part because 9/11 had hit the fashion industry hard and Gucci had yet to fully recover from the dent in profits.

As a result, Stella McCartney Ltd. went through a change in oversight when Gucci announced in November that Marco Bizzarri would become the label's new chief executive. Bizzarri's appointment was meant to quell rumors that the McCartney brand was barely staying afloat. Bizzarri stated that his focus would be to develop the still young label into a strong global brand. That same month, more information was released to the public. Sales had

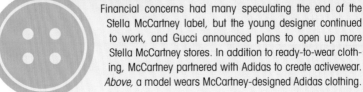

Financial concerns had many speculating the end of the Stella McCartney label, but the young designer continued to work, and Gucci announced plans to open up more Stella McCartney stores. In addition to ready-to-wear clothing, McCartney partnered with Adidas to create activewear. *Above,* a model wears McCartney-designed Adidas clothing.

risen by 50 percent, and a plan was in motion to open new Stella McCartney stores in Milan and Paris within the next three years. Overall, the company was on track to set worldwide sales totaling more than £20.8 million (about $34.5 million at the time).

Even with this positive spin, the first two years at Gucci had not necessarily been easy for the Stella McCartney brand or for the designer herself. The label lost $4.8 million its first year and $7.8 million its second year. Meanwhile, Chloé sales the first year after McCartney's departure went up 60 percent. When someone is an adult child of one of the world's biggest celebrities, sometimes people revel in that person's failures. The Brit designer's detractors, and there were many to choose from, began speculating that the outstanding success of Chloé during McCartney's reign was due to Phoebe Philo, a friend and colleague that McCartney had brought on board as a design assistant after her appointment as chief designer. Philo had become Chloé's head when McCartney left to start her own label. Now she was being perceived by some as Chloé's true talent.

WORKOUT WEAR GETS A NEW LOOK

McCartney continued to do everything she could to bring her brand to the forefront. In September 2004, she began a lucrative long-term deal with athletic shoe and clothing giant Adidas, bringing to market the critically acclaimed line "adidas by Stella McCartney," which now boasts women's activewear for gym, yoga, tennis, running, swimming, dancing, golfing, and winter sports.

McCartney's goal with the line was to change what she currently saw out in the market; she felt women's sports clothes were much too basic and the designs much too similar. She wanted to give women activewear clothing that they would want to wear because they felt good about how they looked in it.

The "adidas by Stella McCartney" line debuted at select Adidas flagship stores in February 2005 and, although sporting wear, the clothes—including reversible jackets, tight-fitting gym tops, limited edition yoga shoes, and boxer-style swim robes in hues of pink, lemon, and gray—still showed McCartney's definite stamp. There were loose sweatshirts featuring drawstrings at both the neck and hem or embroidered embellishments and sweatpants created jodhpur style and adorned with zippers near the ankles. There was something else very Stella McCartney about them, too—the price; her sports pieces cost more than most typical workout wear. Regardless of the cost, the collection proved so popular that its distribution was soon extended into both Europe and Asia.

ONE TINY DEBUT

On February 25, 2005, McCartney made another debut just days before her next anticipated collection was expected to hit runways that March. She and husband Alasdhair brought their first child, a son, into the world. The baby was born in London at St. Johns and St. Elizabeth Hospital and named Miller Alasdhair James Willis. He weighed 7 pounds, 7 ounces (3.37 kilograms) and arrived three weeks ahead of schedule. Baby Miller's early arrival so close to collection time had the fashion world in a bit of a frenzy. McCartney's publicist, however, was able to assuage people's concerns, telling Vogue.com UK, "Stella worked on and was able to complete the collection before giving birth." McCartney's work ethic and commitment to her clothing line was evident; she was viewing digital photos to give the sign-off on final outfits only hours before her labor began.

The show went on without McCartney in attendance. In general, it was well received, with a few fashion writers saying that it was a more mature and confident collection. Cathy Horyn of *The New York Times* said, "The collection was solid, especially the oversize knitwear and the slouchy wrap coats, and if she [McCartney] has lost some of the girl flash, she has gained brand identity." Another reporter, Alex Kuczynski, who reviewed the Stella McCartney store in April for *The New York Times,* called the spring-summer collection lighter and less theatrical.

Kuczynski described some of the pieces of the popular collection, which could be found inside the New York store with its

McCartney and her husband, Alasdhair Willis *(above, carrying their daughter)*, married in 2003 and welcomed their first child in 2005, right before an important fashion show. McCartney had worked throughout her pregnancy, up to the point of delivery, in order to ensure her collection would debut on time.

metal rod dividers, ivory-colored screens, and Lucite shelves. There were carefree dresses meant to slip off the shoulder while worn, as well as simple and elegant dresses of sheer, white cotton. Buying a simple cotton voile dress would mean taking almost $800 out of one's purse, and a skirt of linen and lace would set a customer back $3,165. McCartney's well-known suits were on display, too. Pants retailed at anywhere from $500 to $800. Jackets, sometimes featuring linings of vivid colors, cost over $1,000. Rap-star–looking gold Adidas tennis shoes with plastic and mesh were being sold for $230, and a batik print doctor's bag went for $545.

PARIS ONCE MORE

McCartney took her act back to Paris at the beginning of October 2005 to show off her spring 2006 collection. Creating a cohesive collection is only part of the hard work of owning a label; putting on a stellar show to get people excited about the clothes is all-important, too.

McCartney chose a ballroom at a luxury hotel for her 10 A.M. event. The models sashayed down a catwalk of white vinyl under the room's domed ceiling and were surrounded by walls of mirrored and ornately sculpted panels. Guests, such as famous French film stars, watched from elegantly designed chairs as the models wore fashions in white, pale blue, and gray that the collection notes described with words like *easy, relaxed,* and *inner confidence.*

While the models may have moved fluidly one after the other in a seamless presentation, backstage it was a different matter altogether—chaos ruled as it often does behind the scenes. As reggae music played from a boom box, almost 140 people swarmed in the backstage area that had been divided into two distinct sections—one for simply the clothes, one for all the mirrored makeup tables and the show's 22 models. In addition to McCartney, her own staff of 12, and the models, there were 13 hairstylists, 16 dressers, 26 makeup artists, 26 photographers, 4 security guards, 4 caterers, 4 producers, 3 public relations people to handle the doors,

A good fashion show requires the work of hundreds in order to seem effortless. Backstage, people are often working at a frenzied pace to ensure that the models are styled correctly, the VIP guests are in the best seats, and the show is running smoothly. *Above,* McCartney adjusts an outfit backstage at her spring/summer 2005 show.

1 stylist and 2 assistants, 1 casting agent and his 2 assistants, and 1 seamstress, not to mention a few family members roaming about.

McCartney responded to the frenetic atmosphere by telling *New York Times* reporter Guy Trebay, "I'm not really sure why I'm in this business at the moment. You should ask me after the show, when we see if they like it. At the moment, I'm like, 'Get me . . . out of here.'"

COLLABORATING WITH H & M

Once again, in 2005, McCartney found herself following in the footsteps of her one-time critic, designer Karl Lagerfeld. The previous

Selling Smart or Selling Out?

McCartney's partnership with H & M was not without controversy in the fashion world. One view taken by many high-end designers is that creating such affordable, consumer-friendly collections can devalue the exclusive brands they have worked so hard to establish, even if only a one-time deal. And H & M in particular has had people in the industry taking sides. The chain's accessible "fast fashion" is viewed by many designers as a detriment to the sale of their own distinguished, high-end clothing.

It is possible that McCartney felt pressure to begin doing these select licensing deals with mass-market companies like Adidas and H & M. In 2004, a nonamicable change in leadership took place at the Gucci Group. It saw the exit of both Tom Ford—one of McCartney's champions—and Domenico de Sole. Robert Polet stepped in as the new chief executive and quickly began drawing lines in the sand to improve Gucci's overall sales. He set forth an ultimatum that even the small brands under the Gucci umbrella, including Alexander McQueen and Stella McCartney, be profitable by 2007. Although McCartney's brand was growing, that growth was costing dollars. The $39 million business had not yet turned a profit, due to the monetary investment needed to open the three brand stores in New York, London, and West Hollywood.

Even if looked down on by some designers, such large-scale partnerships are often quite lucrative. In joining with H & M, not only was McCartney guaranteed to make money, she would receive a great deal of exposure for her relatively young brand. In an October 2005 *New York Times* article, McCartney explained her reasoning behind the H & M licensing deal: "I would be lying if I didn't say this helped financially. But I would never jeopardize my brand for any amount of money. We're asked to do this on a regular basis, and the majority of them have been turned down. . . . The days of elitism in fashion are over. . . . It is a misconception of the luxury goods industry that the top end of ready-to-wear is not always accessible. I want people to understand what I do, instead of only seeing something in a glossy magazine."

year, Lagerfeld had done a collection exclusively for Swedish-based retailer H & M. The Lagerfeld collaboration proved hugely successful for the "cheap chic" chain. Lagerfeld had a 50-year high-fashion reputation, so people viewed his collection for H & M as a couture bargain, forming long lines outside of stores in New York and Europe in anticipation of the clothing's release. McCartney did not have the same number of years of experience, but undoubtedly, H & M hoped to repeat the success with the famous up-and-comer.

Reportedly, McCartney made $1 million for the deal, which required less than a week of her time. She spent two days choosing designs and discussing which fabrics and trim should be used. Another day was spent selecting the right colors. Then two more days were taken to complete three fittings. The result was undeniably Stella McCartney. McCartney herself described it as a greatest hits collection that took the looks from her past work and recreated them for the more frugal customer by using basic fabrics and having them made in Romania.

Whereas her sweaters could easily sell for $1,000, one knit cardigan in the H & M collection was long and chunky with a double zip closure and wide ribbing at the hemline, which meant it could be worn as a scrunched-up sweater or left to hang as a short dress. The price? About $920 cheaper than the original—only $79.90. Other items in the 45-piece collection of clothing and accessories included a brown, baggy trench coat with a lining of pink mesh, skinny pants and narrow zipped jeans, a cropped jacket of gray plaid with yellow-trimmed pockets and buttonhole, and graphic T-shirts with line drawings and adorned with chains, rhinestones, and embroidery.

The collection arrived in 400 H & M stores on November 10 and sold out in minutes, making McCartney's success with this venture unquestionable. Later, the must-have pieces could only be found for much higher prices on Internet auction sites like eBay. McCartney's rock star one-off collection for H & M proved to be a real coup that helped the retailer's sales soar.

6

The Brand Branches Out

At the beginning of 2006 in February, a big change came for Stella McCartney Ltd. when James Seuss vacated his executive position to join the revered company Harry Winston, and McCartney's husband, Alasdhair, was announced as the company's director. Stella McCartney Ltd. was now a family affair.

STELLA McCARTNEY HITS THE SLOPES

More changes came in March that year when McCartney's partnership with Adidas took the form of a skiwear collection that made its debut, appropriately, in the mountains of Aspen, where ice-skaters, wearing muted shades of dusty rose, dark chocolate, dark bone, and rosewood, danced across a glossy rink for reporters. The ski pants and jackets were both feminine and practical—a winning combination of Stella McCartney aesthetic and Adidas sportswear technology.

In addition to ski pants and soft-shell jackets, the collection included a one-piece ski jumpsuit, a padded ski coat with a removable vest, and McCartney's take on the moon boot—which could be worn in two ways since the interior booty could be removed and worn alone as after-ski footwear. Much attention was given to the details, with pieces including such features as pockets for MP3 players, cell phones, goggles, and money, in addition to holders for ski passes and lipstick.

McCartney, herself a ski and snowboarding enthusiast, was excited by the opportunity to create something that she felt was missing in the market. Fashionunited.co.uk ran this quote from *Women's Wear Daily*: "I've been desperate to get some

Many designers hoping to create a lasting impression opt for a more theatrical version of a runway show. McCartney presented her Adidas skiwear line with ice-skaters and skiers in Aspen, Colorado, in 2006.

chic-looking skiwear. I think it's been missing. I've gone to buy ski clothes, and I've found it really difficult to find something I wanted to wear. Everything was always badly cut, and the fit was appalling. I don't want to look like a man when I'm skiing. Something about it was always quite wrong to me."

ACCESSORIES GO VEGAN

McCartney made progress with her desire to cut the use of leather in fashion by launching a line of vegan-friendly accessories in June 2006. Accessories had always been a part of the designer's collections, but as yet, there had never been an official Stella McCartney accessories line of its own.

Using a combination of human-made and natural materials like canvas, nylon, velvet, and vinyl, the items were of course more than just animal-lover friendly; they were attractive enough that a person did not need to be vegan to appreciate their style. The site inhabitat.com reported that in a recent interview, McCartney had said, "It's surprising to me that people cannot get their heads around a non-leather bag or shoe. They already exist out there, but unfortunately designers feel that they have to slap a leather trim or sole on them. People need to start looking at the product, and if they like it, that's all that matters. If it has an ethical or ecological edge, that's a huge bonus. We address these questions in every other part of our lives except fashion. Mind-sets are changing, though, which is encouraging."

The line, produced entirely in Italy, was extensive and included a set of nine handbags all named after breeds of horses—one of McCartney's passions. At $1,395, the set's Appaloosa bag was a vintage-looking number in shiny patent faux leather with a subtle logo stamped on its bronze medallion. The subtle logo was markedly different from the heavily logo-laden bags of many other labels. The collection also included belts, luggage, jewelry, purses, and shoes, all available at the Stella McCartney stores in New York, Los Angeles, and London as well as other select shops. The least expensive of the jewelry items was $95, and the shoes could cost as much as $1,595 for an embroidered pair.

Chief executive Bizzarri said that even before this launch, 16 percent of the Stella McCartney business was accessories—like 2005's sellout thigh-high boots that McCartney believed most women did not even realize were a nonleather product. Bizzarri estimated that within the next three years, accessories might account for 30 percent of the label's sales.

SCENTS AND SKIN CARE

Maybe as an outlet for her mix-and-match persona, McCartney released a second fragrance in September 2006 called "Stella In Two." The perfume was unique in that it separated out the two key notes found in the original Stella scent. The peony scent was captured in liquid form and the amber fragrance as a solid perfume. The two could then be worn to match a woman's whim at any time: either one or the other separately or both layered together for a completely different effect.

In addition to the launch of a second perfume, McCartney and husband Alasdhair had something else to be excited about later that year. On December 8, the designer gave birth to the couple's second child and first girl, Bailey Linda Olwyn Willis. She was a 7-pound, 14-ounce (3.57-kg) bundle of happiness whose middle name was a tribute to McCartney's beloved mother, Linda.

Now a mother with two children, McCartney continued to branch out her business into new areas, debuting CARE, the first luxury organic skin-care line, in collaboration with YSL Beauté in 2007. The designer, however, made no rush to get the product to market; instead, she took three years to work on the line, getting the formula for each product just right. She describes the line, which is made of 100 percent organic active ingredients, as modern in both its philosophy and aesthetic and created it with the hope that it might become, for some people, their first step in making responsible choices in their daily routine.

Like her mother, McCartney has always been a passionate animal rights activist and vegetarian. Her firm beliefs have led to her unique relationship with leather-loving fashion company Gucci, one she hoped would allow her to become an educator in vegan fashion. McCartney's accessories line has proved to the fashion industry that shoes and purses do not need to be made of leather to be fashionable.

THE LABEL AND LINGERIE

Life was going well for McCartney in 2007. She was living in two homes—one in Worchester and one in London—and not only had she begun a new skin-care line, but in August she announced plans to launch a lingerie collection, which she would continue to work on into 2008. The designer believed a foray into lingerie was a natural progression for her since she had used it as an influence in her designs ever since her graduation collection at Central Saint Martins. Not to mention, she had fallen in love with beautiful French slips with their inlays and handwork at an early age, so developing a lingerie line was something she had always wanted to do.

The collection, which would be done in partnership with Bendon, a New Zealand company, would align with the clothing of her label. McCartney intended the lingerie pieces to have a natural, confident, and modern aesthetic that used fabrics such as silk, organic cottons, and georgette silk chiffons—a sheer type of silk. These intimate pieces would be produced in the subtle hues that had become a Stella McCartney signature, soft shades like cream, blue, pearl gray, and vintage pink.

A VERY GOOD YEAR

The year 2008 was especially good to the 37-year-old McCartney. First, she gave birth to a baby boy—Beckett Robert Lee Willis—on January 8. In keeping with the tradition of honoring family members through her children's names, the middle name Lee stood for McCartney's late maternal grandfather, Lee Eastman.

Now a mother of three, McCartney kept her career momentum going by continuing with her string of successful partnerships and collaborations. She debuted a limited edition travel collection for the bag and luggage company LeSportsac in the spring of 2008. The designer was excited to work with LeSportsac because she admired the company's history of crafting nonleather goods. This collaboration—like previous ones with H & M and Adidas—could only help promote the McCartney brand. Prices for her label's

ELEMENTS OF STYLE

I am in the fashion business but I feel when I design I'm in the business of trying to figure out what people want and why they want it. One of the main reasons that I do work in the fashion industry is because I'm intrigued about why people choose certain clothes to reflect their mood. It's not about going to fabulous parties. I'm very much interested in details, and to me details that are not even apparent sometimes are as much about fashion as a bright fuchsia puffball cape.

—*Stella McCartney, http://www.StellaMcCartney.com*

accessories were top dollar, but this 18-month partnership (with the possibility for extension) would make products with the Stella McCartney name and cachet available to younger fans with smaller budgets. It also got the designer into a new realm of accessories that catered to busy women. The deal would benefit LeSportsac as well. Fashionunited.co.uk ran a quote from president and CEO Steve Jacaruso, who said his company wanted to "tap into Stella McCartney's creative vision and take [LeSportsac] to the next level of high-end design and style."

The much-anticipated collection of 30 to 40 pieces included travel bags, baby luggage, and totes for mothers with babies and young children. The items could be found in the New York and Los Angeles Stella McCartney shops, in high-end boutiques, and department stores around the world, as well as online. Prices ranged from $200 to $250.

GOING BALLISTIC OVER A BRA

In September 2008, McCartney almost became embroiled in a legal dispute over a single piece from her lingerie collection. The well-known animal-rights designer was shocked when she saw a model wearing a black lace bra of her design under an expensive mink coat in an advertisement in the pages of *Vogue* magazine. (The insult may have been doubled by the leather belt cinching the coat around the model's waist.) The ad was for Hockley, a London Mayfair boutique that specializes in fur. Lending out pieces of a collection for use in photo shoots was nothing out of the ordinary for Stella McCartney Ltd., but in this case, the apparel was apparently lent to a stylist "in good faith." It was obvious that McCartney—a firm PETA (People for the Ethical Treatment of Animals) activist—never would have approved something from her line appearing in an ad promoting the wearing of fur.

An unnamed source from the London Stella McCartney store told the *Daily Mail* that "Stella went absolutely ballistic when she saw it [the ad]." The source had never seen McCartney so upset, and the designer had said heatedly that she would sue.

Hockley soon found out about McCartney's dismay and quickly issued an apology, saying they would not run the ad again—a costly decision since the photo shoot had probably rung in at £10,000 (about $17,800 at the time) alone and the ad placement in the high-profile September issue of *Vogue* at another £26,400 (about $47,000 at the time). The *London Evening Standard* ran the Hockley spokesman's statement: "Hockley is aware of Stella McCartney's views and is respectful of them. This was an unfortunate mistake and Hockley would not intentionally make anyone feel uncomfortable. Hockley both requested and was told that the item was a vintage piece and apologises for any embarrassment caused to Stella McCartney. It is not Hockley's intention to use the image again."

A FINANCIAL COUP

The year came to a close with a business high in October that marked an important milestone for Stella McCartney Ltd.—the label cleared its first serious profit with pretax earnings of £1.1 million (about $1,645,000 at the time). This figure did not even reflect the company's U.S. stores or wholesaling revenue; it accounted for

An Award-Winning Woman

In the summer of 2003, McCartney was given an honorary doctor of laws degree at the University of Dundee in England. Making the announcement in March, a school spokesperson said in the Guardian.co.uk, "We just decided we would like to honour her because of her contribution to fashion and textiles, because we have so many textiles students here." That summer, McCartney met with design students attending the university's Duncan of Jordanstone College of Art and Design. In the ceremony oration, the speaker had this to say of the British designer's career and work: "Today the University of Dundee is acknowledging Stella's formidable achievements with the award of an honorary degree. This

McCartney's discipline and skills have enabled her to achieve her childhood dream of being recognized for her work, not her lineage. She has received multiple awards and honors in fashion and in activism.

is in recognition of the contribution she has made to international fashion design and for the way she has become a role model to students in Art Colleges across the UK and the world, as an individual, as a creative influence and in her professionalism."

Here is a list of the accomplished fashion maven's other honors:

VH1/Vogue Designer of the Year Award (2000)
Woman of Courage Award (2003)
Glamour Award for Best Designer of the Year (2004)
Star Honoree at the Fashion Group International Night of the Stars (2004)

(continues)

(continued)

> Organic Style Woman of the Year Award (2005)
> Elle Style Award for Best Designer of the Year (2007)
> British Style Awards Best Designer of the Year (2007)
> Spanish Elle Awards Best Designer of the Year (2008)
> First-Ever Green Designer of the Year at the Accessories Council Excellence Awards (2008)
> Honored by the Natural Resources Defense Council for her support of environmental causes (2009)
> Named one of *Time* magazine's 100 Most Influential People (2009)
> Honored as one of *Glamour* magazine's Women of the Year (2009)

only the London shop and licensing profits. The label's sales for the fiscal year totaled £11.27 million (about $16,848,00 at the time).

Running a profitable business is no easy feat, and it took Stella McCartney Ltd. six years and £14 million (about $20,930,000 at the time) in losses to start turning such a profit. The label had been in the black for the first time the previous year, but the amount was negligible. The woman whose designs *Vogue* editor in chief Anna Wintour once called "trashy" and proclaimed made her ashamed to be British now had more than just a fashion career, she had a credible and commercially successful label.

THE FASHION SHOWS GO ON

Reveling in her label's financial success, McCartney revealed her new spring collection in Paris on October 2. At the time, because the economy was doing so poorly around the globe, not many designers were taking any risks with their lines. McCartney did much the same, but still managed an excellent job of creating the right mix. The collection featured a few pieces not just the average woman could wear, along with the practical, wearable fashions that her business depended on. The jumpsuits she had become famous for were a big part of the mix. There was one of dark green silk with short bottoms rather than full-length pants, and another to be worn as an evening outfit in the style of a tuxedo. A sequined catsuit was also featured, along with loose-fitting cashmere jumpers. Her swimwear that season got people's attention since it was defined by the full, rather than skimpy, bottoms most designers were turning out. Dresses included a blue chambray mini with cutout detail, a gray strapless evening gown of shantung silk, and several of the more casual T-shirt variety. The jackets—in beach-inspired colors of sea green, pink, and sand—were often oversized or the opposite, cropped and boxy. There were jersey vests in a pale peach color called "flesh" in the show notes and loose-fit pants to accompany them.

The activist designer's collection and its beach-holiday theme garnered more stellar reviews—once again without the use of any leather or fur—something that made McCartney unique.

7

Activist and Advocate

Throughout her life, Linda McCartney was a strong advocate for many social and environmental causes. She was also well known for her vegetarian lifestyle, which included writing a number of successful vegetarian cookbooks. Her first, *Linda McCartney's Home Cooking*, published in 1989, became the United Kingdom's largest-selling vegetarian cookbook and a best seller in the United States. Linda even created a line of frozen vegetarian meals that became hugely popular, with 5 million sold in the United Kingdom by the fall of 1991. Meals of her design are even menu items at the Hard Rock Café in London.

Linda's ideals and work had a great influence on her daughter and how she would approach her own life's work. In fact, in a 2009 article in *The Guardian*, the McCartney daughter was called "one of Britain's most outspoken vegetarians." McCartney talked about her vegetarian lifestyle in a 2006 *London Evening Standard* article: "For me, vegetarianism is based on ethics. It's how I was brought up. My mum was very vocal and we were all educated to understand why we weren't eating meat. But actually, now I look at it from all different angles, I think it's very wrong to have the mass murder, every single day, of millions of animals. I find something wrong with that on a spiritual level, an environmental level and an ethical level."

Even early on in her career, McCartney refused to compromise such ideals for the love of fashion. She worked for a brief stint at Patou, a maker of expensive custom clothing, but the experience did not last long. McCartney did not feel comfortable working for someone who used fur. But the activist designer is well aware that her lineage entitled her to the luxury of sticking to her guns when it came to her early work with Gucci—a fashion house recognized for its use of leather. In the back of her mind, she always knew that she could remain adamant about not using leather for her label because if the Gucci Group at some point became unhappy with her decision and dropped her from its lineup, she would always have her parents and their support to fall back on.

LEADING THE WAY

McCartney uses mainly cotton and silks in her clothing designs. And her refusal to use leather in her collections has led her to pursue alternative and pioneering means of making fashion accessories. On the soles of her vegan-friendly shoes, one will find the phrase "Suitable for vegetarians." McCartney says that for bags and shoes alone, 50 million animals are killed each year, not to mention the incredible amount of energy that is wasted to raise animals that will eventually be destroyed in the name of fashion.

McCartney refuses to design clothes made from animal products. Her collections reflect her dedicated views as an animal-rights activist, and she instead uses faux fur, vinyl, and other alternative textiles to replace or mimic materials derived from animals.

ELEMENTS OF STYLE

I am a fashion designer. I'm not an environmentalist. When I get up in the morning, number one I'm a mother and a wife, and number two I design clothes. So the main thing I need to do is create, hopefully, exquisitely beautiful, desirable objects for my customer. That's my job, first and foremost. If I can make you not notice that it happens to be out of biodegradable fake suede, if I can make you not notice that it hasn't killed cows or goats or unborn baby lambs, then I'm doing my job. There should be no compromise for you as a customer. I don't want to do scratchy, oatmeal-coloured things, that defeats the object. And sometimes . . . I try really hard, but if now and again I have to dye a bag using chemicals that are not as low in environmental impact as I'd like, in order to get a brighter colour, then I will do that.

—*"Stella McCartney: 'Fashion People Are Pretty Heartless'"*
by Jess Cartner-Morley in the Guardian.

As an advocate for animal rights in the fashion industry, McCartney is a fish fighting to swim upstream and says many of her fashion colleagues find her a "pain" and think of her as a "mad hippy" for espousing her views. Even fairly early in her career in the year 2000, the designer made a short video titled "Stella McCartney's Fur Farm Expose." Needless to say, it was not well received by her fashion industry colleagues. In a 2009 *Guardian* article, she says, "People in fashion just don't want to hear the messages. I find it astounding, because fashion is supposed to be about change—I mean, we're supposed to be at the cutting edge! I can only think they don't care as much as people in other industries. So, yes, I think people in fashion are pretty heartless. . . . They are heartless. They must be! Why on earth would they use fur and leather otherwise? There's no excuse for fur in this day and age. Baby kids are boiled alive. Foxes are . . . electrocuted. If that's not heartless, what is?"

TAKING IT PERSONALLY

McCartney's the first to admit that she is not perfect when it comes to living up to her ideals, coping with things like having only one recycling bin at home and still flying on planes, but she strives to make inroads wherever she can. For instance, the company responsible for producing her fragrances, at McCartney's instruction, is not allowed to use genetically modified materials in the perfume's creation and cannot use plants that are harvested by child workers or that appear on the list of endangered species.

Stella McCartney's Tips for Eco-friendly Living

1) If you want to help animals, the best way is not to eat or wear animal products and to encourage others to do the same.
2) Use green power whenever possible.
3) Use and reuse biodegradable bags whenever you shop.
4) Recycle glass. Recycling one bottle saves enough energy to run a computer for 25 minutes.
5) Paint to save energy. If you live in a cold climate, paint your house a dark color. If you live in a hot climate, paint it a light color. (Dark colors absorb the sun's rays, while light colors reflect them.)
6) Help charities rather than adding to landfills. Donate unwanted clothes, electronics, toys, and other goods to thrift stores, so your donations can have a second life.
7) Recycle your aluminum. It takes 95 percent less energy to recycle one can than to create one entirely new can.
8) Fill your home with plants. They help brighten your mood and also act as natural "air conditioners."
9) Compost your food waste. Then you can use it as nutrient-rich soil for your yard or garden.

And whenever possible, the idealistic designer tries to practice what she preaches. Stella McCartney Ltd. is a carbon-neutral organization. At both her home and design studio operations in the United Kingdom, she uses Ecotricity—a British electric company that uses the money customers spend on electricity and invests it in forms of clean power such as wind energy. The Stella McCartney store in Mayfair, London, runs on electricity generated by wind power. McCartney also developed 100 percent biodegradable corn shopping bags. And although they will dissipate

10) Watch your use of water, especially letting faucets run. Letting the water run continuously while you brush your teeth wastes more than 132 gallons (500 liters) a month or 1,584 gallons (5,996 liters) a year!

11) Insulate the walls of your home—it's the most cost-effective way to save energy in the home.

12) Make the switch to energy-saving compact fluorescent bulbs. They use a fraction of the electricity of regular bulbs and last much longer.

13) Turn off lights and electronics when not in use.

14) Put a plug in each of your sinks as a reminder to turn off the faucet.

15) When taking a shower or bath, turn down the temperature.

16) Take a shower instead of a bath; showers usually use only two-fifths of the water that a bath uses up.

17) When buying new appliances and electronics, look for energy-efficiency logos.

18) Once your electronic gadgets are fully charged, turn the power off if not in use.

19) Use both sides of any sheet of paper.

20) If you have a garden or lawn to water, do it early in the morning or late in the evening, so the water is not wasted through evaporation.

For more tips, see the Stella McCartney Web site.

within one year, meaning zero pollution, she encourages people to reuse them as much as possible anyway. Her company also recycles, in total more than 2 tons (1.8 metric tons) of paper each year. And whenever she needs to call a taxi, she uses a car service that features hybrid vehicles.

McCartney's views on the environment became even more important to her after the birth of her son Miller. In a 2006 *London Evening Standard* interview, she said, "I found that when you have a baby, they are so pure and untouched that a car goes past and you look at all the pollution and you really want to protect them." That year, this feeling led her to buy a Lexus RX 400h, the first truly luxury hybrid SUV available. The vehicle combines a gasoline-fueled V6 engine with a battery pack and electric motor generators.

ORGANIZING FOR CHANGE

The eco-conscious designer likes to be an example and hopes to encourage others to follow her environmentally friendly ways. On her company site for the Stella McCartney line, she devotes a page to a variety of charities and nonprofits that she believes are doing good work for the Earth and its people: Adventure Ecology, Animal Aid, Children's Action Network, Fauna and Flora International, the Humane Society of the United States, Kanye West Foundation, Marine Connection, Natural Resources Defense Council (NRDC), Oceana, Peace One Day, and PETA.

McCartney has strong ties to PETA, an organization her mother worked on behalf of as well. One of the ways the designer worked to help PETA in 2007 was to take fur protests online and into a new age through a virtual summer event. From July 12 to July 29, people could sign on and visit a virtual island created to look like a Stella McCartney–inspired English countryside, complete with stables, picnic tables, and even a Linda McCartney veggie-burger stand. Visitors could become Second Life characters who could rent roller skates, bikes, and rowboats. They could also

People for the Ethical Treatment of Animals (PETA) is one of the largest animal-rights advocacy groups in the world. Known for their dramatic, and often controversial, efforts to educate the public about the advantages of a vegetarian lifestyle, PETA boasts celebrity members such as McCartney and her father.

wear antifur accessories as well as a T-shirt with the slogan "I'd rather be pixilated than wear fur"—a take on the famous PETA tagline "I'd rather go naked than wear fur." In a topiary maze on the island, characters could find messages and explore McCartney's cruelty-free skin-care line, CARE. Tree houses on the island were a place to watch some of the designer's fashion shows. But most importantly, characters were able to donate virtual money that the PETA group could then exchange for real currency. Part of the serious fun included a contest for new PETA slogans. What was the prize? Two tickets to the Stella McCartney spring 2008 show in Paris, one of her highly sought Appaloosa bags from her accessories line, and an entire set of her CARE skin and body products.

In 2009, McCartney, along with her sister Mary and father, Paul, took another step for change and started a campaign called Meat Free Monday. According to the Web site, it is "an environmental campaign to raise awareness of the climate-changing impact of meat production and consumption." The site goes on to say that a majority of people are unaware that the production of livestock is responsible for 18 percent of global greenhouse gas emissions, which is more than the entire transport sector.

McCartney lives her beliefs and is not afraid to share her thoughts with others. In *The Guardian,* McCartney stated, "The way my parents brought me up to see the world is still absolutely key to what I am about. The beliefs I was raised with—to respect animals and to be aware of nature, to understand that we share this planet with other creatures—have had a huge impact on me." Most likely, just like her mother, she will remain an activist and advocate for both animals and the environment all her life.

8

McCartney Continues
Making Her Way

McCartney had a real coup in 2009 when she was named one of *Time* magazine's 100 Most Influential People under the category Builders and Titans. She was the only person in the fashion industry to make the list in a year that included such far-ranging personalities as President Barack Obama, Amazon.com founder Jeff Bezos, and entertainers like Zac Efron and Tina Fey. McCartney's recommendation for the list came from friend Gwyneth Paltrow, who said in the magazine, "Everything about Stella McCartney is authentic. Her red hair is her own. She has real guts. She means what she says. Sometimes it's even a bit scary: she somehow works tirelessly to create the chic looks that have made her a fashion icon and yet still manages to be home with her three beautiful children at the same time. She laughs really hard. And she is a vegetarian. I mention this because you cannot accurately characterize Stella McCartney, 37, without underlining that she is a vegetarian. Always has been. And even if you are not interested in being a vegetarian, somehow Stella gets you to believe. She manages to convince you (never sanctimoniously, never from a soapbox) that killing animals is needless and cruel and bad for the environment.... Stella is an uncanny mélange of passion and cool, and that is her deadly weapon."

McCARTNEY KIDS AROUND

The women's wear designer took on a new challenge that year as well, inking a deal to create a line of children's clothing for GapKids and babyGap. In a June 2009 press release, Marka Hanson, president of the Gap brand, said of having McCartney on board, "Her experience as a parent and designer are sure to delight both kids and parents alike."

Once immersed in the project, McCartney found the experience took her a bit out of her comfort zone. What she discovered was that her usual method of designing clothing that she and her friends would like did not translate into designing for young children. McCartney mentioned that her four-year-old, Miller, had a certain sweater that he refused to wear, so she knew from her own

---

ELEMENTS OF STYLE

I definitely took a couple of things that are totally Stella and reduced them down [for the upcoming GapKids collection], because I know that's what I would want if I was one of the parents buying this. I'd be like, "I want that, but little." But the challenge was that this goes up to age 12, so you're not just designing for the mums and dads. My eldest is four and a half and suddenly, he has all these opinions on what he wants to wear. Oh, and we did have jumpsuits to start with, but you know, kids have to pee.

—Stella McCartney in the Guardian.co.uk

Designing children's clothing for the Gap gave McCartney a new challenge as a designer. She used her own children as inspiration. Her limited edition collection at GapKids quickly sold out.

experience as a mother that kids want to wear what they want to wear—not necessarily what Mommy and Daddy want them to wear.

Miller ended up playing a role in the Gap line's designs. McCartney took into account his likes and dislikes in creating the clothes. In the end, her boys' clothing line covered a variety of themes like robots, monsters, and superheroes. For the girls' items, McCartney borrowed a bit from her own tomboy childhood, creating hoodies of gray cashmere and motorcycle details, typical Stella McCartney military jackets shrunk down to kid size, and a sweater with an intarsia leopard pattern. Pieces of her children's Gap collection, which became available in stores at the beginning of November, ran anywhere from $14 to $128. The line was a sell-out success, with even adult women getting in on the action and buying the largest-sized pieces to wear themselves!

A PERFUME GETS SCENT-SATIONAL

During the GapKids line creation, McCartney also planned the release of her third perfume in late August; however, the launch was almost upset by Ali Hewson, wife of U2 front man Bono. Hewson was involved with a cosmetics business called Nude Brands Limited (NBL) that produced a variety of products, including cosmetics, perfumes, and a body product line called Nude Skincare. When Hewson got wind that McCartney's new perfume was to be called StellaNude, she took legal action, trying to get an interim injunction to block the fragrance's release under that name. Described as "investor and muse" in legal documents, Hewson was actually co-owner of the registered trademark NUDE (in all capital letters). The McCartney perfume was set to be labeled as STELLANUDE on its packaging.

On August 20, however, the court decided that Hewson's company had no grounds for an injunction, and McCartney was able to launch StellaNude that weekend as planned. Court judge Mr. Justice Floyd was quoted in the *London Evening Standard* as saying, "I have come to the conclusion that the balance of injustice in this case requires me to refuse the injunction. It seems to me that, in this particular case, the likely damage to SML [Stella McCartney Limited] and L'Oreal [McCartney's partner] if an injunction is wrongly granted outweighs the damage to NBL if it is refused. The effect of an injunction wrongly granted against SML would be to cause a massive disruption to their business, and probably cause them to abandon use of the brand altogether." Stella Steel had won yet another battle.

DOING GOOD

McCartney had another Bono-related experience later in December of that year—this one much more pleasant and for a good cause; she designed a T-shirt for World AIDS Day. Her design was part of the Gap (PRODUCT) RED collection, a merger of fashion and activism. (PRODUCT) RED is a charity led by Bono and created in the hopes of eliminating the plague of AIDS in Africa.

The T-shirt, which went on sale December 5, was a simple, classic white one—a Gap standard—but embellished with a printed design of a layered red beaded necklace. Given her previous success with GapKids, the T-shirt was made available in sizes for both women and girls. Fifty percent of the profits were given to the Bono charity.

THE RUMOR MILL GETS IT WRONG

Toward the end of 2009, a news item emerged that McCartney was about to collaborate with British cult singer and fellow vegetarian Morrissey for a line of leather-free shoes. News spread quickly in both the fashion and music worlds. The *UK Daily Mail* originated the story, complete with a quote from McCartney that said, "I'm working with Morrissey on a line of leather-free shoes which I'm really excited about. We are still in early stages, but the shoes could be launched next year."

But apparently something was amiss with the reporting. Not long after the story spread to other papers, Internet sites, and blogs, McCartney's team put a post on her Facebook page refuting both the story and the quote's validity: "Stella is a fan of Morrissey but those rumors of collaboration for a shoe line are simply not true." The celebrated designer had to clear up yet another rumor around the same time. McCartney assured British magazine *Grazia* that talk of a design collaboration between her and popular singer Leona Lewis was strictly a rumor and held no truth. McCartney, now famous in her own right, was finding more and more that as her business grew, so did the rumors and gossip.

A DESIGNER IN WONDERLAND

In January 2010, McCartney took a turn toward the fanciful. She teamed up with Disney to design limited edition costume jewelry inspired by the studio's upcoming film *Alice in Wonderland* from director Tim Burton. The fashion maven was in good company; jewelry designer Tom Binns himself created pieces featuring teacups and hearts, while cosmetics favorite Urban Decay produced a limited edition eye shadow palette with a pop-up scene from the *Alice in Wonderland* book, and nail giant O.P.I. released four exclusive colors: "Off with Her Red," "Thanks So Muchness!," "Absolutely Alice," and "Mad as a Hatter." McCartney's contribution included two unique pieces: a necklace and bracelet, which could be found on sale in her stores at month's end for $425 and $395 respectively.

DEATH OF A FRIEND

But just as it can happen in anyone's life, McCartney felt the sting of tragedy in February 2010 when friend and fellow fashion designer Alexander McQueen was found dead in his home by apparent suicide at the age of 40.

Much of the fashion world came out on February 24 to pay tribute to the acclaimed designer at a service held at Saint Paul's Church in London; McQueen fashions were de rigueur of many at the somber ceremony. McCartney attended along with mutual friends Naomi Campbell and Kate Moss.

MARCH MADNESS

That March, McCartney paid tribute to her now departed friend, stating in her show notes, "This show is dedicated to my hubby, kids, family, team and friends. This one is also for Lee [McQueen's first name]....You're missed!" That ready-to-wear collection for fall/winter 2010 received rave reviews. Inside the opulent setting of a Parisian opera house, models flaunted no-nonsense day wear along with stunning evening wear.

Neutral colors like gray, black, and camel dominated—especially in the reinvented men's bespoke wardrobe pieces—but then flashes of color as seen in a silk fuchsia cocktail dress appeared in dramatic fashion.

Attendees were treated to day wear pieces including fisherman-style oversized knits, a large-ribbed V-neck cardigan, quilted jackets, big parkas, and a variety of minidresses—one with oversized camel-

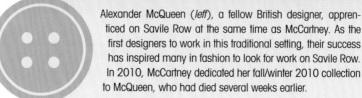

Alexander McQueen (*left*), a fellow British designer, apprenticed on Savile Row at the same time as McCartney. As the first designers to work in this traditional setting, their success has inspired many in fashion to look for work on Savile Row. In 2010, McCartney dedicated her fall/winter 2010 collection to McQueen, who had died several weeks earlier.

Alexander McQueen

Born Lee Alexander McQueen on March 17, 1969, the man who would later become the bad boy of fashion had a modest start in life, raised by his mother and cab driver father. By age 16, McQueen knew that fashion was his destiny and quit school to apprentice, like McCartney, on Savile Row, with both tailors and costumers. (In fact, they trained there at nearly the same time, although neither knew it then.) Later he went on to work with designer Koji Tatsuno and at age 21 went to Milan to work with Romeo Gigli.

Like McCartney, Alexander McQueen attended Central Saint Martins, but he had started there with the intention of learning to be a pattern cutter. He went on, however, to earn a master's degree in fashion design. His graduation show took place in 1992—the year McCartney joined the school. He, too, had a much-hyped show, and his entire clothing collection was bought by Isabella Blow, a British eccentric and a big name in the world of fashion magazines. She is quoted on Vogue. co.uk as saying, "When I said, 'I know this sounds a bit weird but I want

and-black stripes. There were also items like a clean-lined cashmere coat, nicely fitted trousers, and a sleeveless taupe jacket that reviewer Gianluca Longo described as being "as sexy as a dress."

The dresses often made use of sequins, silk, and lace. A sleeveless, high-neck dress in burnt orange had a definitive 1960s feel to it. There was a one-sleeved dress in black organza. Others featured low-draped backs, long trains, and subtle lace over nude fabric. *Vogue* fashion writer Dolly Jones called McCartney's efforts, "a beautifully managed collection with all the Stella quality but slightly less of the pizzazz." She also commented, "Stella always has her eye on comfort as an inherent factor of style."

to buy the whole of your collection,' Alexander McQueen offered to sell me a coat for £350 (about $600 at the time). I said, 'That's a lot for a student.' And he said, 'But I made it.' In the end I bought it all for £5,000 (about $8,700 at the time) but it took me a long time to pay for it."

The designer, who began his own self-titled label, became known for a "brutally sharp" style that garnered a lot of attention and acclaim, as well as for his theatrical shows. In 1997, McQueen was named designer in chief at French house Givenchy. With a bit of impertinence, he called the couture house's founder "irrelevant." Not surprisingly, his first collection for the couture house failed miserably. The fashion world is rarely forgiving, but somehow, McQueen managed to stay afloat—maintaining respect in the industry and staying with Givenchy for three years.

In 2000, he signed a joint-venture contract with Gucci—again, just like McCartney—which allowed the designer much more creative freedom. By 2007, he had shops around the world, and his unique designs could be seen out on the red carpet, worn by stars like Nicole Kidman and Sarah Jessica Parker.

The four-time British Designer of the Year was found dead of an apparent suicide in his Mayfair home on February 11, 2010. His mother, Joyce, whom he adored completely, had died just a few days previously. He was only 40 years old, but left a legacy of completely original fashion.

But McCartney had even more to offer that March. The celebrity fashion designer's GapKids debut had been a tremendous success, and as a result, she was tapped for a second collection. The designer held a preview event in London mid-month. Some of the adults who came could be seen wearing the girls' military jacket from her previous collection. Friends like Kate Moss and other U.K. celebrities were on hand, most with kids in tow to enjoy the treats provided, like ice cream and jelly (British for Jell-O). An article on Elle.co.uk said big hits of the collection, which was due to hit stores at month's end, were sure to be the nautical-striped tops, denim shirts, anchor-print sweaters, and patterned sundresses.

Success and status in the fashion industry never comes easy, but McCartney's hard work, dedication, and unique views have made her one of the most respected designers of her generation. Her successful mix of activism and fashion, vintage and modern, feminine and masculine, has influenced fashion trends and pushed the public to a higher awareness of environmental causes.

FASHION FOREVER

Born with a famous name, McCartney has overcome criticism and skeptics and has turned that name into an international brand, creating clothes that are coveted by the world's most fashionable women. She has gone from a one-woman design shop in her own apartment to a greatly desired designer label with 14 stores, including major ones in Manhattan, London, Los Angeles, and Paris. Her more recent store openings have included such far-away destinations as Bahrain, Dubai, Kuwait, and Qatar in the Middle East; Bangalore, India; Hong Kong and Shanghai, China; and Tokyo, Japan. Her collections have grown to include women's ready-to-wear, accessories, eyewear, fragrance, lingerie, and skin care. These collections can be found in more than 50 countries in both specialty shops and department stores around the world.

McCartney has been a breakthrough in what has long been a male-designer-dominated fashion industry. She has also been a breakthrough as a strong advocate for cruelty-free clothing. Her refusal to use leather or fur in her products is a novelty in the world of fashion. No doubt, the outspoken designer will continue to work on behalf of animal rights and to promote vegetarian living—thus, carrying on the compassionate work so important to her mother.

Though her career has had both its share of highlights and disappointments, there can be no question that the woman known as Stella Steel will continue to please fashionistas everywhere with her signature style of sharp tailoring, natural confidence, and feel-good femininity. The McCartney name will not be known only for legendary music; now, it will also be known for legendary fashion.

Chronology

1969	Beatle Paul McCartney and photographer Linda Eastman marry.
1971	SEPTEMBER 13 Stella Nina McCartney is born in London, England, shortly after the breakup of the Beatles.
1986	At age 15, interns with famed designer Christian Lacroix.
1995	Earns BA from prestigious fashion college Central Saint Martins; gets attention for her graduation show that includes her supermodel friends.

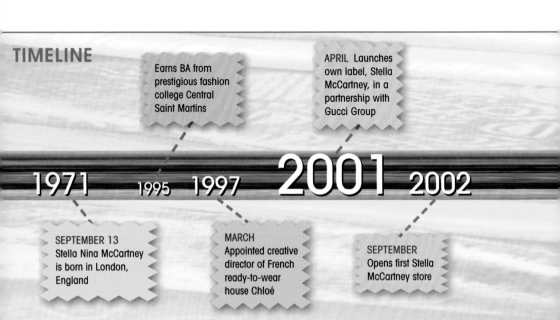

TIMELINE

Earns BA from prestigious fashion college Central Saint Martins

APRIL Launches own label, Stella McCartney, in a partnership with Gucci Group

1971 1995 **1997** **2001** 2002

SEPTEMBER 13 Stella Nina McCartney is born in London, England

MARCH Appointed creative director of French ready-to-wear house Chloé

SEPTEMBER Opens first Stella McCartney store

1995	Launches small line of her own from home; line is simply called Stella.
1997	MARCH Appointed creative director of French fashion house Chloé.
1998	APRIL Suffers a great loss when mother, Linda, dies of cancer.
1999	JANUARY Makes well-publicized quote about being tired of criticism for getting to where she is only because of her famous father.
	FALL Speculation begins that she may be leaving Chloé.
2000	OCTOBER Wins VH1/Vogue Designer of the Year Award.
	DECEMBER Designs friend Madonna's wedding dress for marriage to Guy Ritchie.
2001	APRIL Launches own label, Stella McCartney, in joint venture with Gucci Group.

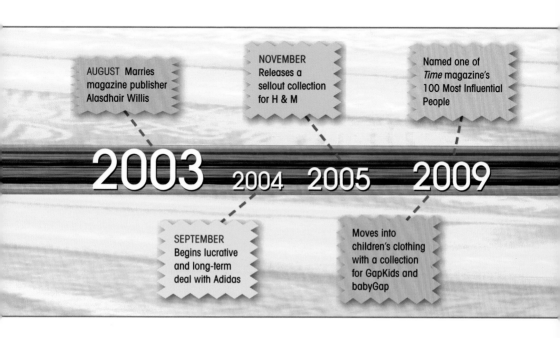

AUGUST Marries magazine publisher Alasdhair Willis

NOVEMBER Releases a sellout collection for H & M

Named one of *Time* magazine's 100 Most Influential People

2003 2004 **2005** **2009**

SEPTEMBER Begins lucrative and long-term deal with Adidas

Moves into children's clothing with a collection for GapKids and babyGap

LATE SUMMER/FALL Begins dating magazine publisher Alasdhair Willis.

OCTOBER First collection for Stella McCartney label debuts in Paris to lackluster reviews.

2002 JUNE 11 Father, Paul McCartney, marries Heather Mills, and reportedly Stella and sister Mary are not pleased.

SEPTEMBER Opens first Stella McCartney store in New York's meatpacking district.

2003 Receives the Woman of Courage Award for work in support of cancer awareness.

MAY Opens second Stella McCartney store in Mayfair, London.

AUGUST Marries Alasdhair Willis in a ceremony on a Scottish isle.

SEPTEMBER Expands her brand by launching Stella perfume.

OCTOBER Opens third store in West Hollywood, California.

2004 Receives Glamour Award for Best Designer of the Year.

SEPTEMBER Begins long-term deal with Adidas; collection is called "adidas by Stella McCartney."

2005 FEBRUARY 25 Gives birth to first child, a boy, Miller Alasdhair James Willis.

Receives the Organic Style Woman of the Year Award.

NOVEMBER Releases a sellout one-off collection for clothing retailer H & M.

2006 SEPTEMBER Launches another new fragrance, "Stella In Two."

DECEMBER 8 Gives birth to a second child, a girl, Bailey Linda Olwyn Willis.

2007 Receives more awards—both the Elle Style Award and the British Style Award for Best Designer of the Year.

In collaboration with YSL Beauté, debuts CARE— the first luxury organic skin-care line

2008 **JANUARY 8** Gives birth to her third child, a boy, Beckett Robert Lee Willis.

MARCH Stella McCartney Ltd. records its first serious profit since launching.

Works on a limited edition travel collection for LeSportsac.

Receives even more awards—Best Designer of the Year at the Spanish Elle Awards and Green Designer of the Year at the Accessories Council Excellence Awards.

SEPTEMBER Becomes enraged when a piece from her lingerie collection is used in an ad to sell a fur coat.

2009 **MARCH** Honored by the Natural Resources Defense Council.

Is named on *Time* magazine's list of the 100 Most Influential People.

Moves into children's clothing by designing collections for GapKids and babyGap.

AUGUST Releases new perfume, StellaNude; U2 front man Bono's wife tries to sue over the use of the word *Nude* in the perfume's name.

2010 Designs a limited edition necklace and bracelet inspired by Tim Burton's *Alice in Wonderland* film.

FEBRUARY Attends the funeral of friend and fellow fashion designer Alexander McQueen.

MARCH Shows off autumn/winter collection in Paris.

Glossary

aesthetic A guiding principle in matters of artistic beauty and taste; artistic sensibility.

apprentice A person who learns a trade by working for someone in that trade.

batik A fabric printed using a specific Indonesian hand-printing method that involves putting a coating of wax on the part of the textile not being dyed.

bespoke Clothing that is made to order; custom-made.

biodegradable Capable of being broken down, or decomposing, by the action of living organisms.

chambray A fine cloth of cotton, silk, or linen often with a plain weave and a colored warp and white weft.

couture High-end clothing created by designers that is usually custom made.

intarsia A knitted design that resembles a mosaic and can be seen on both sides of a fabric.

interim injunction A court order that forbids something from happening until a specified date.

jodhpurs Riding pants cut full through the hips and close fitting from the knee to the ankle.

one-off Limited to a single time, occurrence, or instance.

ready-to-wear Clothing that is made in standard sizes and ready to wear immediately after purchase.

topiary maze   A maze created from live hedges that are specifically clipped and trimmed into a maze shape.

voile   A fine soft, sheer fabric often used in summer clothing for women.

Bibliography

"The 2009 *Time* 100." Time Web site. Available online. URL: http://www. time.com/time/specials/packages/completelist/0,29569,1894410,00. html.

"Alexander McQueen Biography," The Biography Channel.co.uk. Available online. URL: http://www.thebiographychannel.co.uk/ biographies/alexander-mcqueen.html.

"And I Love Her: Sir Paul McCartney Pulls Out All the Stops for Daughter Stella's Wedding on a Scottish Isle." *People*. September 13, 2003. Available online. URL: http://www.people.com/people/archive/ article/0,,20141056,00.html.

Armstrong, Lisa. "Stella Nova." *New York*. August 25, 2002. Available online. URL: http://nymag.com/nymetro/shopping/fashion/features/n_7580.

"Avenue of the Americas: Cats and Hats." *FT.com*. September 19, 2002.

"Biography for Stella McCartney," Internet Movie Database. Available online. URL: http://www.imdb.com/name/nm0565383/bio.

Carlin, Peter Ames. *Paul McCartney: A Life*. New York: Simon & Schuster, 2009.

Cartner-Morley, Jess. "Stella McCartney: 'Fashion People Are Pretty Heartless.'" *Guardian*. October 5, 2009. Available online. URL: http:// www.guardian.co.uk/lifeandstyle/2009/oct/05/stella-mccartney- fashion-heartless.

"Central Saint Martins," London Fashion Week Web site. Available online. URL: http://www.londonfashionweek.co.uk/designer_profile.aspx? DesignerID=66.

"Central Saint Martins College of Art and Design," Fashion Design Runway.com. Available online. URL: http://www. fashiondesignrunway.com/central-saint-martins.php.

Chambers, Veronica. "She Grooves. Will She Go?" *Newsweek*. October 18, 1999.

Cohen, Lara, and Jill Ishkanian. "Stella's Star-Studded Wedding." *Us Weekly.* September 15, 2003.

"The College: Our History," Central Saint Martins Web site. Available online. URL: http://www.csm.arts.ac.uk/csm_history.htm.

Cornita, Jenny. "Award-Winning Style." *Us Weekly.* November 6, 2000.

Craik, Laura. "Skin Colours and Classic McCartney Tailoring at Breezy Show in Paris." London Evening Standard. October 2, 2008. Available online. URL: http://www.thisislondon.co.uk/standard/article-23563014-skin-colours-and-classic-mccartney-tailoring-at-breezy-show-in-paris.do.

Craven, Jo. "Who's Who: Isabella Blow." *Vogue* UK Web site. April 22, 2008. Available online. URL: http://www.vogue.co.uk/biographies/080422-isabella-blow-biography.aspx.

————. "Who's Who: Stella McCartney." *Vogue* UK Web site. April 22, 2008. Available online. URL: http://www.vogue.co.uk/biographies/080422-stella-mccartney-biography.aspx.

Cruz, Clarissa. "Dress Right: The VH1/Vogue Fashion Awards—Gisele Bundchen and Men of Honor's Cuba Gooding Jr. Hosted the Style Awards Ceremony." *Entertainment Weekly.* November 3, 2000. Available online. URL: http://www.ew.com/ew/article/0,,278294,00.html.

Danyelle, Jill. "Stella McCartney Vegan Fashion," Inhabitat Web site. November 26, 2006. Available online. URL: http://www.inhabitat.com/2006/11/26/stella-mccartney-vegetarian-fashion.

Davis, Johnny. "The Fashion Stars of Central Saint Martins." *Observer.* February 7, 2010. Available online. URL: http://www.guardian.co.uk/lifeandstyle/2010/feb/07/central-saint-martins-louise-wilson.

Dera and Associates, Inc. "Linda McCartney," The Virtual Museum of the City of San Francisco. 1997. Available online. URL: http://www.sfmuseum.org/hist6/lindabio.html.

"Dundee Honours Stella." *Guardian.co.uk.* March 3, 2003. Available online. URL: http://www.guardian.co.uk/education/2003/mar/03/students.uk1.

"During Childhood Stella McCartney Was Unaware That Her Dad Was a Beatle," Exposay.com. Available online. URL: http://www.exposay.com/during-childhood-stella-mccartney-was-unaware-that-her-dad-was-a-beatle/v/15878.

"Faces of the Week: Stella McCartney," BBC News Web site. Updated December 12, 2003. Available online. URL: http://news.bbc.co.uk/2/hi/uk_news/magazine/3313867.stm.

Fashion United Web site. Available online. URL: http://www.fashion united.co.uk/news/stella.htm.

Gorman, Carrie. "Uncomplicated Elegance." *Elle* UK Web site. March 9, 2010. Available online. URL: http://www.elleuk.com/news/Fashion-News/stella-s-uncomplicated-elegance/(gid)/520142.

Harris, Paul, Richard Simpson, and Anny Shaw. "Kate Moss, Naomi Campbell and Stella McCartney Pay Respects to Alexander McQueen at Intimate Funeral Services." Mail Online Web site. February 25, 2010. Available online. URL: http://www.dailymail.co.uk/news/article-1253724/Alexander-McQueen-funeral-Kate-Moss-Naomi-Campbell-Stella-McCartney-pay-respects.html.

Hayt, Elizabeth. "A Night Out with Stella McCartney; Designer on the Run." *New York Times.* December 12, 1999. Available online. URL: http://www.nytimes.com/1999/12/12/style/a-night-out-with-stella-mccartney-designer-on-the-run.html?scp=1&sq=stella%20designer%20on%20the%20run&st=cse.

Helligar, Jeremy. "The McCartney Family Feud." *Us Weekly.* July 8/July 15, 2002.

Horyn, Cathy. "Essence of Chanel: Coco? Karl? Both." *New York Times.* March 5, 2005. Available online. URL: http://www.nytimes.com/2005/03/05/fashion/shows/05dres.html.

Hyde, Marina. "Stella McCartney v Ali Hewson: Who Has the Right to Be 'Nude'?" *Guardian.* August 14, 2009. Available online. URL: http://www.guardian.co.uk/lifeandstyle/lostinshowbiz/2009/aug/14/stella-mccartney-ali-hewson-nude.

Jones, Dolly. "Stella McCartney: Show Report Autumn/Winter 2010–11." *Vogue* UK Web site. March 8, 2010. Available online. URL: http://www.vogue.co.uk/fashion/show.aspx/catwalk-report/id,8874.

Keeps, David A. "Sir Paul's Little Girl Opens in Los Angeles." *New York Times.* October 5, 2003. Available online. URL: http://www.nytimes.com/2003/10/05/style/sir-paul-s-little-girl-opens-in-los-angeles.html?scp=1&sq=sir%20paul%27s%20little%20girl&st=cse.

Kuczynski, Alex. "Simple Store to Clear Your Mind, and Your Wallet." *New York Times.* April 21, 2005. Available online. URL: http://www.nytimes.

com/2005/04/21/fashion/21critic.html?_r=1&scp=1&sq=simple%20 store%20to%20clear%20you%20mind&st=cse.

"Linda McCartney Biography," Biography.com. Available online. URL: http://www.biography.com/articles/Linda-McCartney-246040.

Longo, Gianluca. "Now Stella Cuts Her Collection from Wardrobe of a Fella." *London Evening Standard.* March 8, 2010. Available online. URL: http://www.thisislondon.co.uk/fashion/article-23813111-now-stella-cuts-her-collection-from-wardrobe-of-a-fella.do.

Low, Valentine. "Mother Inspired Me, Says Stella." *London Evening Standard.* Updated January 26, 2006. Available online. URL: http://www.thisislondon.co.uk/showbiz/article-21542564-mother-inspired-me-says-stella.do.

Michaels, Adrian. "Stella Qualities." *FT.com.* September 20, 2002.

"Morrissey Not Working with Stella McCartney on Shoe Line." Spinner. Available online. URL: http://www.spinner.com/2009/12/14/morrissey-not-working-with-stella-mccartney-on-shoe-line.

Mower, Sarah. "Spring 2006 Ready-to-Wear: Stella McCartney." Style. com Web site. October 6, 2005. Available online. URL: http://www.style.com/fashionshows/review/S2006RTW-SMCCARTN.

Owen, David. "Going Solo." *New Yorker.* September 17, 2001.

"*People* Gets Madonna Wedding Information." *USA Today.* December 27, 2000. Available online. URL: http://www.usatoday.com/life/music/madonna/mad06.htm.

"The PETA Files: Updates and Full Schedule for PETA/Stella McCartney Second Life," PETA Web site. July 12, 2007. Available online. URL: http://blog.peta.org/archives/stella.

PR Newswire. "Glamour Names First Lady Michelle Obama, Stella McCartney and Rihanna Among 2009 Women of the Year," November 9, 2009. Available online. URL: http://www.prnewswire.com/news-releases/glamour-names-first-lady-michelle-obama-stella-mccartney-and-rihanna-among-2009-women-of-the-year-69559037.html.

————. "Winners Undraped at the 2000 'VH1/Vogue Fashion Awards,' Hosted by Cuba Gooding, Jr. and Gisele Bundchen," October 20, 2000. Available online. URL: http://www2.prnewswire.com/cgi-bin/stories.pl?ACCT=104&STORY=/www/story/10-20-2000/0001344806&EDATE=.

Prynn, Jonathan. "Stella's Week Gets Even Better as She Goes into Profit." *London Evening Standard.* October 3, 2008. Available online. URL: http://www.thisislondon.co.uk/standard/article-23563470-stellas-week-gets-even-better-as-she-goes-into-profit.do.

Relax News. "Stella McCartney to Team Up with Morrissey for Vegan Shoe Range." *Independent.* December 1, 2009. Available online. URL: http://www.independent.co.uk/life-style/fashion/news/stella-mccartney-to-team-up-with-morrissey-for-vegan-shoe-range-1832180.html.

Scarff, Liz. "A Stella Career." *Elle* (Canadian Version). Available online. URL: http://www.lizscarff.co.uk/journalism/stella-mccartney.

Sells, Emma. "Stella McCartney Designs for Disney." *Elle* UK Web site. January 13, 2010. Available online. URL: http://www.elleuk.com/news/Fashion-News/stella-mccartney-designs-for-disney.

———. "Stella McCartney's (Gap) RED T-shirt Hits Stores Tomorrow." *Elle* UK Web site. December 4, 2009. Available online. URL: http://www.elleuk.com/news/Fashion-News/stella-mccartney-s-gap-red-t-shirt-hits-stores-tomorrow.

———. "Stella Reveals Her Latest Gap Kids Collection." *Elle* UK Web site. March 17, 2010. Available online. URL: http://www.elleuk.com/news/Fashion-News/stella-reveals-her-latest-gap-kids-collection/(gid)/530971.

Sherwood, James. "Stella McCartney: Don't Call Me Daddy's Girl." *Independent.* March 6, 2005. Available online. URL: http://www.independent.co.uk/news/people/profiles/stella-mccartney-don't-call-me-daddys-girl-527338.html.

Smiedt, David. "Rock Star Daughters: What Would Your Life Be like If Mick Jagger Were Dad?" *Marie Claire.* February 2006.

"Stella McCartney," Encyclopedia of World Biography Web site. Available online. URL: http://www.notablebiographies.com/news/Li-Ou/McCartney-Stella.html.

"Stella McCartney," Running with Heels.com. Available online. URL: http://www.runningwithheels.com/index.php/2009/01/stella-mccartney.

"Stella McCartney: Biography," *Hello!* Available online. URL: http://www.hellomagazine.com/profiles/stella-mccartney.

"Stella McCartney Denies Morrissey Collaboration," NME News. Available online. URL: http://www.nme.com/news/morrissey/ 48841.

"Stella McCartney 'Goes Ballistic' as Her Bra Is Used to Sell £6,500 Mink Coat." *London Evening Standard.* August 9, 2008. Available online. URL: http://www.thisislondon.co.uk/showbiz/article-23530286-stella-mccartney-goes-ballistic-as-her-bra-is-used-to-sell-pound6500-mink-coat.do.

"Stella McCartney: Honorary Degree Oration," University of Dundee Web site. Available online. URL: http://www.dundee.ac.uk/pressoffice/ grad2003/stellalaureation.html.

"Stella McCartney: Label Overview." *New York.* March 16, 2010. Available online. URL: http://nymag.com/fashion/fashionshows/designers/ bios/stellamccartney.

"Stella McCartney Perfume Block Bid Fails." *London Evening Standard.* August 20, 2009. Available online. URL: http://www.thisislondon. co.uk/standard/article-23734800-stella-mccartney-perfume-block-bid-fails.do.

"Stella McCartney's Linda Inspiration," Monsters and Critics Web site. July 6, 2008. Available online. URL: http://www.monstersand critics.com/people/news/article_1415212.php/Stella_McCartney_ s_Linda_inspiration.

"Stella's Baby Boy." British *Vogue* Web site. March 1, 2005. Available online. URL: http://www.vogue.co.uk/news/daily/2005-03/050301-stellas-baby-boy.aspx.

Support Meat Free Monday Web site. Available online. URL: http://www. supportmfm.org.

"Top Designers: Stella McCartney Bio," FashionTV Web site. Available online. URL: http://www.ftv.com/fashion/page.php?P=2765.

Trebay, Guy. "Fashion Diary; Now Opening for Business: McCartney." *New York Times.* September 20, 2002. Available online. URL: http://www.nytimes.com/2002/09/20/nyregion/fashion-diary-now-opening-for-business-mccartney.html?scp=1&sq=now%20 opening%20mccartney&st=cse.

————. "The Young Designer Who Worked in a Shoe." *New York Times.* October 8, 2005. Available online. URL: http://www.nytimes. com/2005/10/08/fashion/shows/08DIARY.html.

Watson, Shane. "24 Hours with Stella McCartney." *Harper's Bazaar.* September 2002.

White, Constance C.R. "Patterns: Chloe's New Chief Designer." *New York Times.* April 15, 1997. Available online. URL: http://www.nytimes. com/1997/04/15/style/patterns-606154.html.

Wilson, Eric. "By Kids, for Kids, via Mom." *New York Times.* October 22, 2009. Available online. URL: http://www.nytimes.com/2009/10/22/ fashion/22ROW.html.

————. "The 3 Faces of Stella." *New York Times.* October 27, 2005. Available online. URL: http://www.nytimes.com/2005/10/27/fashion/ thursdaystyles/27STELLA.html?_r=1&scp=1&sq=the%203%20 faces%20of%20stella&st=cse.

Zimbalist, Kristina. "Women in Luxury: Stella McCartney." *Time.* September 4, 2008. Available online. URL: http:// 205.188.238.181/ time/ specials/2007/style_design/article/ 0,28804,1838865_1838857_1838733-2,00.html.

Further Resources

BOOKS

Carlin, Peter Ames. *Paul McCartney: A Life.* New York: Simon & Schuster, 2009.

Davies, Hywel. *British Fashion Designers.* London: Laurence King Publishers, 2009.

Espejo, Roman, ed. *The Fashion Industry* (Opposing Viewpoints). Farmington Hills, Mich.: Greenhaven Press, 2010.

Newkirk, Ingrid. *The PETA Practical Guide to Animal Rights: Simple Acts of Kindness to Help Animals in Trouble.* New York: St. Martin's Griffin, 2009.

Schoumann, Helene. *Chloé.* New York: Assouline Publishing, 2003.

Ungs, Tim. *Paul McCartney and Stella McCartney* (Famous Families). New York: Rosen Publishing Group, 2004.

WEB SITES

The CarbonNeutral Company
http://www.CarbonNeutral.com

People for the Ethical Treatment of Animals (PETA)
http://www.peta.org

Stella McCartney
http://www.stellamccartney.com

Style.com
http://www.style.com/fashionshows/complete/S2009RTW-SMCCARTN
Click on links on the timeline at the bottom to see reviews and images from McCartney's collections over the years.

Support Meat Free Monday
http://www.supportmfm.org

Picture Credits

Page:

8	Scott Gries/Getty Images
11	Corbis
14	David Montgomery/Getty Images
16	Jan Persson/Redferns/Getty Images
19	BEN STANSALL/AFP/Getty Images
21	Alamy
24	Dan Kitwood/Getty Images
29	JACK GUEZ/AFP/Getty Images
32	Robin Platzer/Twin Images/Getty Images
34	Mario Tama/Getty
38	Dave Benett/Getty Images
43	Serge Benhamou/Prestige/Getty Images
47	Alamy
55	Jennifer Graylock/AP Images
58	Ian Lawrence/Splash News/Newscom
60	Eric Ryan/Getty Images
64	Riccardo Savi/Getty Images
67	Riccardo Savi/Getty Images
71	Corbis
76	REUTERS/Charles Platiau/Corbis
81	Dave M. Benett/Getty Images
85	Nick Harvey/WireImage/Getty Images
89	Dave Benett/Getty Images
92	PATRICK KOVARIK/AFP/Getty Images

Index

A

accessories, 65–66, 75
Adidas by Stella McCartney, 56–57
Adventure Ecology, 80
Alice in Wonderland, 87–88
Anderson, Pamela, 52–53
Animal Aid, 80
animal rights activism, 33, 37, 69–70, 75–77, 82
apprenticeships, 20–22, 90
Auerbach, Frank, 23
awards, 71–72

B

babyGap, 84–85
Banks, Jeffrey, 31
Beatles, 9–10
Bergdorf Goodman, 25, 28
Binns, Tom, 87–88
birth of Stella McCartney, 11
Bizzarri, Marco, 54–56, 65–66
Blanchett, Cate, 52
Blow, Isabella, 90–91
Bono, 86
branding, 40
Branson, Richard, 36
breast cancer, 30–31, 49, 54
Brosnan, Pierce, 51
Burton, Tim, 87–88
buttonholes, 19

C

Campbell, Naomi, 22, 88
cancer, 30–31, 49, 54
carbon neutrality, 79
CARE, 66, 82
Central Saint Martins College of Art and Design, 19–20, 23, 90
Children's Action Network, 80
children's clothing, 84–85

Chloé, House of, 7, 26–30, 31, 33–36, 56
costume jewelry, 87–88
costumes, 49

D

de Rossi, Portia, 53
de Sole, Domenico, 39, 54, 61
Designer of the Year awards, 7
Diaz, Cameron, 36
Duff, Hilary and Haylie, 52

E

Eastman, Linda. *See* McCartney, Linda (mother)
eco-friendly living, tips for, 78–79
Ecotricity, 79
endangered species, 78

F

Fauna and Flora International, 80
fittings, 48
Ford, Tom, 33, 37, 41, 54, 61
fragrances, 51, 52, 66, 78, 85
Freud, Lucien, 23
fur, 37, 69–70, 75, 77

G

Galliano, John, 23
GapKids, 84–85, 87, 91
genetically modified organisms, 78
Gigli, Romeo, 90
Givenchy, 91
Gucci Group
    activism and, 75
    H & M decision and, 61
    McQueen and, 91
    rumors about, 33
    working with, 37–42, 54–56

H

H & M, 60–62
Hanson, Marka, 84
Hewson, Ali, 86
Hockley, 70
Hollywood, store in, 51–54
honorary doctor of laws degree, 71
horses, 65
House of Chloé, 7, 26–30, 31, 33–36, 56
Hudson, Kate, 9, 36
Humane Society of the United States, 80
hybrid vehicles, 80
Hynde, Chrissie, 36

J

Jacaruso, Steve, 69
Jackson, Betty, 18–19
Jackson, Michael, 16–17
Jagger, Mick, 15
jewelry, 87–88
Jolie, Angelina, 49

K

Kane, Christopher, 23
Kanye West Foundation, 80
Kensit, Patsy, 25
Key to the Cure initiative, 49
Kidman, Nicole, 36, 49, 91

L

Lacroux, Christian, 18
Lagerfeld, Karl, 9, 26–28, 37, 60–62
Law, Jude, 49
Le Bon, Yasmin, 22
leather, 33, 37, 65, 75
LeSportsac, 68–69
licensing, 25, 61
Linda McCartney's Home Cooking (McCartney), 74
lingerie, 68, 69–70
logos, 40

M

Madonna, 35, 36, 51
Mazar, Debi, 52
McCartney, Heather (half-sister), 10, 11, 15
McCartney, James (brother), 12, 15
McCartney, Linda (mother)
    death of, 30–31
    early life with, 10–11, 13–15

graduation from Central Saint Martins and, 22–23
    influence of, 44, 74
McCartney, Mary (sister), 11, 15, 43, 82
McCartney, Paul (father), 7, 11–17, 22–23, 42–44, 82
McDermott, Dylan, 52
McQueen, Alexander
    Central Saint Martins and, 22, 23
    death of, 88
    H & M and, 61
    New York and, 46
    overview of, 90–91
Meat Free Monday, 82
Miller, Phillip, 31
Mills, Heather (step-mother), 42–45, 51
Morrissey, 87
Moss, Kate, 22, 51, 88, 91
Moufarrige, Mounir, 26–27

N

Natural Resources Defense Council, 80
New York, store in, 45–48
Nieman Marcus, 25, 28
Nude Brands Limited, 86

O

Oceana, 80

P

Paltrow, Gwyneth, 9, 49, 51, 83
Paris, 59–60
Parker, Sarah Jessica, 91
Patou, 75
Peace One Day, 80
perfumes, 51, 52, 66, 78, 85
PETA, 70, 80–82
Philo, Phoebe, 56
Polet, Robert, 61
(PRODUCT) RED collection, 86–87
profit, 70, 72

R

Ritchie, Guy, 35

S

Saks Fifth Avenue, 31, 49
Savile Row, 20–22, 25, 90
See line, 35
Seuss, James, 46–47, 63
Sexton, Edward, 20–22

shoes, 56
shopping bags, 79–80
skin-care products, 66, 68, 82, 86
Sky Captain and the World of Tomorrow,
  49
LeSportsac, 68–69
sportswear, 56–57, 63–65
"Stella In Two," 66
StellaNude, 86

T

Tatsuno, Koji, 90
Time Magazine, 83
Tokio, 25
Toledano, Ralph, 33
Tyler, Liv, 7, 9, 36, 51

U

Unforgettable Evening event, 54
Universal Design Studio, 46
University of Dundee, 71
Urban Decay, 88

V

vegan-friendly accessories, 65–66, 75
vegetarianism, 33, 52, 74–75, 83–84
Vogue, 19, 69–70

W

wedding dresses, 35, 45, 51
Willis, Alasdhair (husband), 39, 49,
  50–51, 63
Willis, Bailey Linda Olwyn (daughter), 66
Willis, Beckett Robert Lee (son), 68
Willis, Miller Alasdhair James (son), 57,
  84–85
wind power, 79
Wings, 12
Wintour, Anna, 36, 72
Wonder, Stevie, 15
World AIDS Day T-shirt, 86–87

Y

yoga, 49

About the Author

REBECCA ALDRIDGE has been a writer and editor for more than 14 years. In addition to this title, she has written several nonfiction children's books, including titles on Apolo Anton Ohno, Thomas Jefferson, Italian immigrants in America, the *Titanic*, and the Hoover Dam. As an editor, she has had input on more than 50 children's books covering such diverse topics as social activism, vegetarian eating, and tattooing and body piercing. She lives in Minneapolis, Minnesota.